CW00675282

BARBEL MANIA

BARBEL MANIA

Andy Orme

The Crowood Press

First published in 1990 by
The Crowood Press
Gipsy Lane, Swindon
Wiltshire SN2 6DQ

© Andy Orme 1990

All rights reserved. No part of this publication may be
reproduced or transmitted in any form or by any means,
electronic or mechanical, including photocopy,
recording, or any information storage and retrieval
system without permission in writing from the publishers.

British Library Cataloguing in Publication Data

Orme, Andy
Barbel mania.
1. Barbel fishing
I. Title
799.1752

ISBN 1 85223 436 9

Acknowledgements

The author would like to thank Chris Turnbull for his superb
illustrations.

Photoset and Printed in Great Britain by
Redwood Press Limited, Melksham, Wiltshire

Contents

Dedication

This book is dedicated to the people who have helped or inspired me during my academic and angling careers. The biologists include: Mrs Dorothy Parkes (Watford Technical High School), Mrs Cynthia Justice-Mills (Harrow College of Technology and Art), Professor David Nichols (University of Exeter), Professor Clive Kennedy (University of Exeter), Dr Mike Ladle (Freshwater Biological Association), and Dr T. T. Macan (Freshwater Biological Association).

The angling writers who have really got my heart thumping and hands reaching for my tackle are: Martin Gay, Jim Gibbinson, Frank Guttfield, Jack Hilton, Bill Keal, Captain L. Parker, Peter Stone, Fred J. Taylor, Dick Walker and Peter Wheat. Their books and articles influenced me tremendously during my early specimen hunting days and I am eternally grateful to them.

Introduction

British rivers are beautiful and fascinating places to sit beside and the barbel which inhabit them present the angler with a superb quarry. These lovely fish are handsome, powerful and pose an absorbing challenge to expert and novice alike.

It has been my pleasure and privilege to fish in many rivers and to catch a great many barbel from them. This book summarises what I have learned and I present my findings to you in the sincere hope that they will help you derive even more enjoyment from the sport and get more barbel on the bank. Good hunting.

The Passion for Fishing

When I was aged just five, my father took me to the Grand Union Canal at Greenford in London on my very first fishing trip. We caught a netful of beautiful roach and I had such a great time that I could not wait to go again the following weekend.

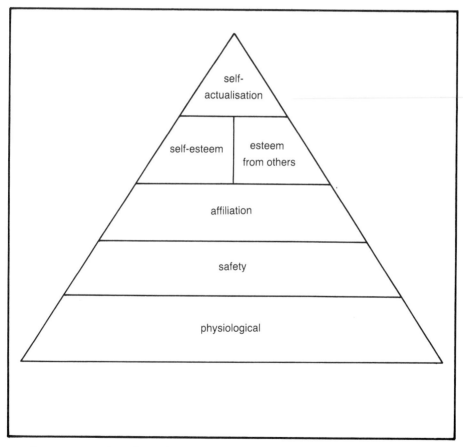

Maslow's Hierarchy of Needs.

*According to market research it is getting fish on the bank
that is one of the main reasons for going fishing and it is
a specimen like this big barbel that will satisfy esteem needs,
according to Maslow.*

That youthful enthusiasm grew over many seasons as I fished the ponds and rivers around Watford. None contained barbel and so I could only dream about these magnificent fish until one day a very kind member of Watford Piscators, Harry Packman, offered to take me to the River Kennet. Harry was a member of the Civil Service Angling Society and they had a lovely stretch of the river at Ham Bridge, Thatcham. My twelve-year-old eyes boggled at the clear water and swaying streamer weed bordering the gravel runs. It was with trembling fingers that I tackled up that morning.

Harry wandered off downstream and, when I thought that he could not see me, I sat on the bridge and cast a lobworm upstream into a shallow run that was technically 'out of bounds'. Almost immediately, the rod slammed over and I was attached to my very first barbel. More by luck than judgement, I extracted it from a variety of weed beds and when, finally, it lay gleaming and gulping in my net I was filled with a mixture of emotions – relief, pride, joy and the anticipation of telling my mates about it back home.

Over many seasons, that youthful enthusiasm grew into such a passion for my sport that I was prepared to sacrifice time, money and even my health in order to catch the fish I had set my sights on. Many a night I would be on a muddy river bank, cold, wet and hungry, the contents of my wallet having been spent on the latest item of tackle or bait for the session. To catch a 10lb barbel and then a twelve-pounder was more important to me than almost anything else in the world.

It is estimated that four or five million people now enjoy fishing in Great Britain. Not all will be as fanatical as I was, but for each one who picks up a fishing rod there must be an underlying reason for doing so and, because I am, by nature, an inquisitive soul, I have tried to analyse these reasons in terms of motivation theory. The late and very great Dick Walker started to explain why people went fishing when he wrote that people need to satisfy inborn hunting instincts, but I think that is only part of the story because fishing has a lot more to offer than that.

A psychologist called Maslow described man as a 'wanting animal' who has a number of needs which he will strive to satisfy. Maslow produced a pyramid of needs. At the bottom he placed the basic needs which are common to all forms of life and at the top he put 'self-actualisation' which he described as the need to fulfil one's inner potential. His theory was that people start at the bottom of the pyramid and strive to move up through the hierarchy. Physiological needs relate to obtaining enough food, drink and shelter in order to survive; safety needs include physical security, job security and a comfortable routine; affiliation needs include social contact,

Getting away from it all helps you to unwind from the stresses of modern society.

friendship and belonging to a group, self-esteem includes the need for self-respect, self-confidence and the need to achieve something worthwhile; esteem from others implies the need for recognition and appreciation for accomplishments and the need for reputation and status; finally, self-actualisation, at the apex of the pyramid, is the feeling of self-fulfilment after the accomplishment of a very demanding and difficult challenge.

Maslow's theory is, of course, a gross over-simplification and does not include such needs as the desire to look at beautiful things or to be in beautiful places or the need to get away from it all. The theory has also been criticised on the grounds that some people will strive to satisfy higher needs and ignore the lower ones. However, like all theories, it is not intended to be regarded as fact – more a means of organising your thinking and generating discussion. One factor which needs to be taken into account is that fishing offers enormous variety and so can satisfy different needs in different people. I recently read some market research on the reasons why people go fishing and found that interpretation of the results in terms of motivation theory was difficult because little account was taken of the different types of anglers. For example, the reasons why specimen hunters, matchmen and 'pleasure' anglers go fishing are likely to vary. The market research showed that, in general, people went fishing mainly to relax, to get fish on the bank and to have the chance to be alone and forget about work and domestic pressures.

Man almost certainly started fishing to fulfil Maslow's base physiological need. Quite simply, a big catch of fish fed the family and kept them alive. In developed Western society we do not have to catch our food so fishing obviously satisfies the higher needs. It is possible that the relaxation offered by the sport contributes to what Maslow described as safety needs because to be able to unwind and relieve stress is vital to good health. Many of our rivers and lakes are wonderful places to sit beside and to be able to rest and watch a glorious misty dawn after a week of hard work is sheer delight. The gurgle of rivers, the scent of wild flowers and the sounds of the waterside make the world a wonderful place to live in. The boss, the mortgage and the phone bill are all forgotten.

Affiliation or social needs are definitely capable of being satisfied by fishing. It is possible to join a huge variety of angling clubs or to simply turn up at a fishery and spend time chatting to like-minded people who share a

Social needs can be satisfied by fishing.

15

love of the sport. For my own part, a great many of my very best friends are anglers and these include the people from my school days, who despite work and family commitments still make time to get together on the bank with their old buddies. There are two clubs specifically for the barbel man – The Barbel Catchers and the Association of Barbel Enthusiasts, the former being an organisation for experienced barbel fishermen and the latter welcoming anyone with an interest in barbel.

Esteem needs, the ones it is easy to deny having, can be satisfied by the capture of a large fish or a bag that wins a match. Let's face it, there is a certain amount of pleasure to be derived from weighing a double-figure barbel in front of an admiring audience of fellows. Self-esteem in the form of self-confidence and self-respect follow but these have to be protected, from friends, who will be convinced that the capture was just a fluke, and also from the miserable knockers, who will be jealous.

It is only recently that I have re-thought the reasons for the success of the bolt rig. This self-hooking rig not only increases your chances of catching something but also increases the sociability of the sport by removing the need to remain glued to your rod. It is possible to fish effectively while enjoying a drink in someone else's bivvy. As long as you can still hear your alarms you know that a take will result in a fish. The bolt rig increases your chance of satisfying esteem needs and social needs, but I would like to say here that I do not agree with the policy of leaving rods to fish for themselves and never do myself.

Self-esteem also includes the need to achieve something worthwhile as a result of skilful performance. Winning matches and regularly catching big fish takes considerable knowledge and practical competence and to know, for example, that you caught a 10lb barbel from a northern river must be very satisfying. Likewise, it must be rewarding to win an open match against a great many competitors or to weigh in more than an England International who sat on the next peg. Fishing is an extremely skilful sport.

At the apex of Maslow's hierarchy is self-actualisation or self-fulfilment. When I set myself the targets of firstly a 10lb barbel and then a twelve-pounder, they were the goals that motivated me to travel to the Hampshire Avon constantly and to fish my heart out. I was in what psychologists call a state of 'drive' and had adopted a pattern of behaviour that would enable me to satisfy the need to achieve something. The angling papers are full of people who have done the same – captors of big fish, winners of matches and triumphant teams. Fishing has provided these people with a means for achievement which is often denied them at work for one reason or another.

To me, the beautiful places are a major attraction of angling.

It is also relevant to look at what de-motivates people in relation to how they spend their time and important factors include monotony and boredom. People get fed up when confronted by lack of variety and challenge and this is often the perception of fishing by the non-angler. I wish I had a pound for every time someone has said, 'How can you sit there for hours on end doing nothing?' Little do these people know that fishermen are in a constant state of anticipation and observation. Of course, from time to time the hours drag but then that happens in nearly every sport.

People are also de-motivated when needs remain unsatisfied. For example, if there are no fish to catch, or the rivers turn into noisy fairgrounds and the people you meet turn out to be aggressive yobbos, then it is a fair assumption that your attention may turn to photography or golf.

There can be little doubt that, despite the simplicity of Maslow's theory it makes some sense in relation to fishing. There is also no doubt whatsoever that our sport has the potential to offer people enormous personal rewards and to contribute greatly to their quality of life. To analyse the benefits in a practical way, rather than a theoretical one, is also useful. Just look at the educational contribution fishing can make to the young. It encourages reading with its many excellent books, magazines and papers, it promotes the study of biology and the countryside and develops an appreciation of the environment and living things. Through the writing of notebooks and fishing logs young anglers develop their writing and personal organisation skills, while learning that success in an activity reflects how much effort is put in, in the first place. Friends are met, new places are travelled to and youthful energy and enthusiasm are channelled in positive and constructive ways.

I do not think my father realised what effect that trip to the Grand Union Canal was going to have, nor Harry Packman, that trip to the Kennet. In the many years that have passed since those trips I have changed and the rivers and lakes have changed, but one thing has remained the same. In the words of Isaac Walton, 'There never was a more calm, quiet, innocent recreation than angling'.

Evolution of a Barbel Fisherman

As a teenager living in Watford with no transport of my own, barbel fishing was never readily available. However, I managed to persuade my parents that Hampshire and Dorset were perfect counties in which to spend holidays and so began a long association with Throop Fishery and the adorable Mrs Sainsbury's Rosalie Guest House. My friends and I caught loads of barbel on those summer holidays and we met many fantastic people, some of whom are now my best friends. During those marvellous days on the Dorset Stour, my personal best barbel steadily rose from those early Kennet tiddlers to almost nine pounds, but of more importance was what I learned about baits, tackle, feeding behaviour, playing, watercraft and other essential facets of the barbel fisher's armoury. I spent many, many hours perched on branches way above the river simply watching fish and their reaction to tackle and bait.

What I failed to achieve was the penultimate aim of all keen barbel men – the capture of a double-figure fish (the ultimate being a record). That was my ambition in my early and mid-twenties but then I had to move to Exeter in Devon which is about as good a place to go barbel fishing as the Sahara Desert is to go skiing.

A move to Reading in Berkshire landed me in the heart of barbel country, within walking distance of the Kennet and Thames in fact, but after two years of fishing these lovely rivers I still had not caught a double. What always rubbed salt into the wound was reading reports in the paper such as, 'Boy's first barbel weighs 11lb'. Inspirational articles by Dick Walker and Peter Wheat turned my gaze to the middle reaches of the Hampshire Avon. Here, it was said, were barbel not just of double figures but leviathans of 15lb or more. That was the sort of stuff that I liked to read and so I resolved to forget all other waters and to concentrate on four or five middle-Avon fisheries.

With my home in Reading each journey to Hampshire involved a 150-mile round trip and considerable expense on petrol and bait. That was a major investment of time and money and so I tried to shift the odds in my favour as far as was possible. My tackle, baits, planning and approach were as perfect as I could make them, but of most importance were my meticulous records of the weather. Wind direction, rainfall and temperature were regularly monitored and before any trip was undertaken I phoned for weather forecasts for the Hampshire and Dorset area. If the elements were not favourable the session was postponed.

Over about a year I made thirty trips to the glorious Avon Valley, caught seventy-three middle-Avon barbel and had a wonderful time in the process. Thirteen fish were over nine pounds and two were over the magical 10lb mark at 10lb 1oz and 10lb 6oz. The latter fish was my first ever double and the story of its capture is told later in this book.

Having got a double under my belt, I now set my sights on a bigger fish and decided on 12lb as a target. I knew a couple of fisheries where such fish existed and firmly believed that with my dedication and approach it would only be a matter of time before I caught one. Such confidence! The value of such optimism is reflected in the tenacity with which one fishes. Every trip I made, I concentrated hard and I expected to land something big.

Six months passed in which I only managed fifteen trips because of pressure of work and other commitments. Twenty-four barbel were landed, five of which were nine-pounders to 9lb 14oz, but the monsters had eluded me. On one trip I had hooked what felt like a huge barbel but had suffered

My first ever barbel from the Kennet at Thatcham when I was about twelve years old.

Throop – one of the fisheries where I learned how to understand barbel.

the agony of the hook pulling out when the fish was just inches from my net. Other fishermen I knew had taken big fish including a twelve-pounder and so I began to question my approach.

January arrived bearing perfect winter barbelling weather – warm westerly winds and masses of lovely rain. Even at night the air temperatures were 10°C and that is amazingly warm for January. A two-day trip was planned, the gear was loaded into the car and then I discovered that my battery was flat. By the time it was removed, recharged and replaced in the car, the morning had evaporated and so I did not get down to the Avon until 3.30 p.m.

The river was brown in colour and flooding over its banks. The water temperature was 9.5°C and so my confidence soared sky-high. After two hours' fishing while sheltering under the brolly from the gales and torrential rain, the rod top pulled round. Five minutes later, following a spirited fight, a good fish lay in the net. One glance was enough. It was another nine – 9lb 3oz to be exact and in beautiful deep-bodied winter condition. 'Good stuff,' I thought, 'they're feeding'.

That evening, I caught no more fish but nearly managed double pneumonia. Soaked to the skin, I sploshed my way back to the car vowing to get a full day's fishing in the next day. After a bite to eat in a local pub I drove to my favourite snoozing spot in the New Forest, reclined the car seats, crawled into the sleeping bag and tried to doze off. Some hope! The rain was falling in buckets and the noise on the car roof was like lead bullets falling from a great height on to a metal baking tray.

Dawn saw me back in the fishery car-park, absolutely shattered and my enthusiasm dented. I can remember thinking how nice it would be to drive home and flop into a lovely warm bed. Somehow, I dragged myself out of the car, loaded the gear on to my back and trudged off on the long walk to the barbel hole. I felt like a zombie. I bowed my head and plodded on.

On arrival at the selected swim, the normal gear was assembled: glass Mk IV Avon, Mitchell Match, 6lb line and a size 4 forged hook presented a large lump of legered chopped ham with pork. About twenty pieces of bait were

An early Throop barbel.

The River Split on the Royalty, scene of many early barbel catches.

carefully scattered in the hole and then I settled down to touch legering. It was still blowing a tremendous gale but I was quite snug under the brolly and the rain had stopped.

After an hour I began to get plucks and very fast, un-hittable (so I found) pulls. I endured these bites for about half an hour before reluctantly scaling down my rig. On went a quiver tip, 3lb line, 12 hook and a small piece of meat. This was light gear for the big fish I was after but I was not certain that barbel were responsible for the bites and in winter the river is relatively clear of weed.

It was about 11 a.m. when I flicked out the modified gear into the swim and, rod in the rests, I sat back not knowing what to expect. Almost immediately the quiver dipped a couple of inches and a strike connected me with something very solid and alarmingly unyielding. How big the fish was I hadn't a clue. Three weeks earlier I had landed a barbel of 8lb 13oz on roach gear and that one had taken me 100 yards down river and almost ten minutes to land. The size of that fish had not been apparent until I saw it.

The fish I was at present attached to, swam slowly and irresistibly out into the main current and sat there. A slight increase in pressure from me

*The School Bridge at Throop where I spent many happy
sessions during college holidays.*

produced no result and so I piled on as much as I dared on the 3lb line. Very,
very slowly I gained a couple of yards but then the rod was wrenched down
and I had no option but to back-wind furiously. Again, I retrieved some line
by straining the light tackle to the limit, and again the response was an
awesome retaliatory surge of power. This give-and-take situation lasted for
about ten minutes but slowly and surely I gained line.

Rather rashly, I bent the Mk IV double and with the line singing in the
wind tried to get the fish to the surface just to catch a glimpse of it. A huge
tail emerged and then, following a massive boil, the fish lunged back to the
sanctuary of the river bed. 'That could be a double,' I said to myself and
suddenly regretted the strain I had put on the flimsy tackle. Suddenly, the
fish decided to swim up and down the hole in mid-water. 'I'm winning,' I
thought, and at last the fish lay on the surface and confirmed its size. Very
gingerly I teased it towards my large net and, with a gasping sigh of relief,
engulfed my prize in the folds of the mesh.

Grabbing the net below the frame, I lifted, and was amazed at the weight
of the thing. Retreating to the safety of the bank I pulled back the dark mesh
and focused my wide expectant eyes on a truly massive fish. It was perfect

24

in every detail and was as deep and thick-set as any barbel I had yet seen. Without more ado I slipped her into the weigh bag and, without zeroing the Avon scales, performed a rough weighing. My heart missed a beat when I looked at the dial.

Almost panic-stricken I rushed down the bank to ask two other barbel fishers to witness an accurate weighing. They duly obliged and the pointer went past the 10lb mark, past the 11lb and 12lb marks and on past the 13lb mark to rest at 13lb 12oz. The bag was weighed at between four and five ounces and so I called the fish 13lb 7oz.

After a photo session I realised that the long fight and stress of handling had taken its toll. There was no way I was going to allow that magical fish to suffer and so for fifteen minutes I nursed her in shallow water willing her to regain the will and stamina to survive back in the flooded river. Slowly but surely, feeble struggles turned to savage lashes of her tail and finally I released her, savouring the magnificent sight of her swimming powerfully off into the river's depths.

'Thirteen pounds and seven ounces.' If I said that to myself once that afternoon, I said it a thousand times. That was in between bouts of singing

The view of the Avon that greeted me at dawn a few hours before I caught my thirteen-pounder.

and other acts of euphoria. I even gave the nuisance swans some bread instead of the usual verbal abuse. After almost two years, 46 trips and 98 other middle-Avon barbel I had at last climbed the barbel fisher's Everest and I am not ashamed to say that I had tears of joy in my eyes.

One nagging doubt remained in my mind. Were the scales accurate? They were about fourteen years old and had not been tested for some time. Next day I took them to the Department of Trading Standards to either confirm or deny my fears. 'Scales of this age,' I was told, 'usually go soft and result in overestimates'. That was definitely not what I wanted to hear and I had to wait an agonising two hours for the results of the test. 'Remarkably accurate,' was the decision. 'Accurate to within half a division which is equivalent to half an ounce'. I could have kissed him. I have never beaten that lovely fish but have caught a great many more barbel, several of them being doubles.

Barbel Biology

One of the major benefits of biological knowledge is its application to fishing. Understanding something of the structure, functions and behaviour of your quarry, will undoubtedly lead to more fish on the bank and greater enjoyment of your sport. This chapter briefly describes the biology of the barbel and concentrates on those aspects of most importance for an angler planning to catch them – location and feeding behaviour.

CLASSIFICATION AND GENERAL BIOLOGY

The scientific name of our quarry is *Barbus barbus* and it is a member of the carp family or Cyprinidae. It is a riverine, bottom-dwelling or benthic,

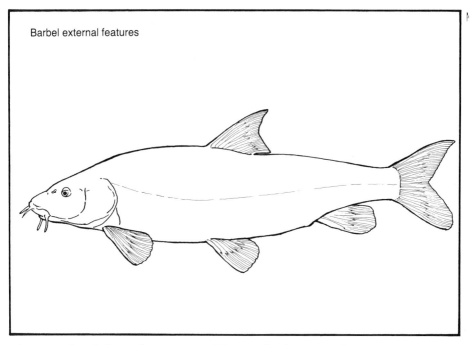

Barbel external features

The streamlined shape, large pectoral fins, underslung mouth and four sensory barbules show how well the barbel is adapted to live in our rivers.

A beautiful streamlined barbel.

fish that grows to about 36in in length and lives for a maximum of fifteen years.

Barbel have a streamlined shape, well-developed pectoral fins and an underslung mouth with four sensory barbules for food detection and identification. They are omnivorous, taking a wide variety of live and dead animal and vegetable material. They have three rows of throat teeth with which to crush these foods.

The species is well adapted to exploiting its environment. In other words, it is well designed to feed, grow and avoid hazards, like predators, in order to breed and ensure that its genetic material will survive in future generations. Any barbel population will display the very common phenomenon of variation. That is individuals within any population will differ slightly in their structure, physiology and behaviour. For example, some barbel in a stretch of river will be short and fat, others long and thin. Some will be more timid than others and will hang back further from a feeder and may be more reluctant to take a bait. The more bold ones will swim straight up to a feeder and start bashing it with their noses in order to get the food out.

NATIONAL DISTRIBUTION

The distribution of this species in Britain has been influenced by two main factors. Firstly, the last ice-age and secondly, man. During the last Pleistocene ice-age much of Britain was covered by ice and the remainder was tundra-like frozen land. Wildlife as we know it today was effectively wiped out by the cold and the sea-level was very low because so much of the world's water was bound up on land in the form of ice. This low level caused the south east of the country to be connected to continental Europe by a land-bridge. About 20,000 years ago the climate became warmer, the ice melted and the sea-level began to rise. Freshwater fish and other aquatic life began to recolonise Britain by swimming up the rivers connected to those of Europe that had not been obliterated by the ice. The Thames, for example, was at that time a tributary of the River Rhine.

About 5,000 years ago Britain was finally cut off from Europe, by the rising sea, leaving barbel populations in only our eastern river systems like the Trent and the Thames. Since then, the distribution of barbel has widened because they have been transported to other rivers by man. In 1896 a London angler, Mr Gomm, introduced about 100 Thames barbel to the Dorset Stour at Iford Bridge. Many of these fish also successfully colonised the Hampshire Avon. Sixty-four Kennet barbel were introduced into the Great Ouse in 1951 by officers of the Great Ouse River Board who were helped by several London anglers. Shortly after that, in 1955, personnel from the river boards and the *Angling Times* introduced many small southern barbel into the Bristol Avon and River Welland. The River Severn received its first official consignment, in 1956, when 500 were released. The River Nene got a smaller batch at the same time.

Many other introductions have been made to several rivers throughout the country, including some non-breeding populations in lakes. Each river has a group of anglers who have specialised in their capture and have become local experts. This information has been documented in The Barbel Catchers' book which is essential reading for any keen barbel man – *Barbel* (The Crowood Press, 1988).

BREEDING AND GROWTH

Barbel breed once a year, usually during May or June, when, I am glad to say, they are protected by the Coarse Fishing Close Season. This is the only time of the season when the two sexes can be distinguished because the smaller males develop tubercles on the gill covers and the females become swollen with eggs. At other times of the year there seem to be no external differences.

The fish seek out areas of clean gravel with a good flow of water. I have watched up to three males in attendance with one female. These suitors seem to stimulate her to lay her eggs by rubbing themselves sinuously along her flanks. The number of eggs she releases varies according to her size and it has been calculated that a 3lb fish will produce about 3,000 eggs and an 8lb fish, about 20,000. These are laid in a shallow depression excavated by the female. The males then fertilise them with their milt after which they are concealed by a covering of gravel. Hatching occurs after about two weeks have elapsed and is influenced by water temperature. Heat will accelerate egg development.

Barbel, like other fish, grow throughout their lives and the size they attain will depend on their genetic make-up and the environment in which they live. Influential environmental factors include food availability and physical conditons like temperature. For example, temperature will have a direct effect on their metabolism because they are 'cold-blooded', and may also affect their food supply. Sexual maturity is reached after four or five years when a female may weigh 3–5lb. The very big fish of 10lb-plus are usually at least eight years old and there are records of fish living for more than fourteen years and attaining weights of over fifteen pounds. The majority of the biggest barbel reported have come from southern rivers like the Dorset Stour and the Hampshire Avon whereas those from the colder northern rivers have been smaller.

So what is a big barbel? Traditionally, a ten-pounder is regarded as the specimen weight to aim for but you must aim lower than this on many waters because such lunkers are either very rare or non-existent. As a general rule, discover the record weight for your local river, multiply it by 0.5 and call that weight 'big', multiply it by 0.7 and call that weight 'very big'. For example, if the biggest barbel you know of from a fishery weighed 14lb, multiplying by 0.5 gives you a 'big' weight of 7lb and multiplying by 0.7, a weight of nearly ten pounds. Comparison of data on the numbers of double-figure barbel reported to the angling press from various rivers illustrates that people fishing in the north of England have a very hard task ahead of them if they are after a double, whereas those sticking a bait in the Hampshire Avon, Kennet or Dorset Stour are in with a good chance of one (*see* page 44).

BEHAVIOURAL ECOLOGY

The distribution of barbel will vary, in time, on a daily and seasonal basis and it will depend on individual fish making decisions largely concerning breeding, feeding and the avoidance of hazards and predators.

All animals try to maintain constant conditions in their bodies so that co-ordinated physiological processes like food digestion and respiration can operate efficiently. Biologists classify animal activities into functional systems for the convenience of study. Behaviour forms part of these systems. The major functional systems are:

1. body regulation and maintenance, e.g. obtaining oxygen
2. feeding
3. hazard avoidance, e.g. sheltering from torrential currents
4. predator avoidance
5. reproduction

If we ignore reproduction, the behaviour patterns adopted by a barbel will promote individual survival. The fish can detect chemical and physical changes in its environment, then assess biological priorities for survival and act or behave accordingly. Modern biological thinking accepts that animals can make rational decisions. They are not simple, programmed robots.

An example would be a barbel sheltering under weed that sees a succulent worm trundling down an exposed gravel run. The decision it has to make is whether to risk exposure to predators by leaving the shelter in order to feed on that item. Before delving more deeply into this subject, it is worth briefly reviewing the barbel's systems that provide it with the information on which to make its decisions about behaviour.

Barbel can see, hear, touch, taste, smell and detect changes in water velocity, temperature and pressure. They have evolved very sensitive and sophisticated systems with which to do this. Barbel have well developed eyes which can see efficiently in low light. Their ears can hear well and it is thought that they use their swim bladders to amplify sound. The nostrils are unlike those of mammals because they are not connected to the respiratory tract but are small pits in the body surface. Another difference is that the fish's sense of smell detects chemicals that are dissolved in water. Some biologists believe that the fish's senses of taste and smell are indistinguishable. Barbel taste potential food items by using sensory receptors on their barbules and lips and in their mouths. Touch receptors are present all over

Watching fish behaviour below the new weir at Throop . . .

their bodies but are also found in high concentrations on the four barbules. These structures are highly sensitive and are particularly important in feeding.

The lateral line system on the barbel's flanks is a complex sensory structure involved in the detection of pressure changes associated with water movement. It provides information for locomotion such as river current velocity, direction and turbulence. There is also some evidence to suggest that it can detect low-frequency sound.

Some fish have been shown to be able to detect tiny changes in temperature and electricity and to use these abilities to detect food. I know of no evidence to show that barbel can do this but that does not mean that they cannot.

FEEDING BEHAVIOUR

Obviously all anglers want their quarry to feed. There are various stages in the feeding process – hunger, foraging or searching, food detection, identifi-

... and again on the Royalty.

cation, selection, ingestion or eating and then satiation and cessation of feeding.

A fish feels hungry when its stomach contents fall to a certain volume and internal chemicals reach certain levels. When it has decided to feed, its behaviour will be affected by the fear of predators and the presence of other fish feeding on the same food. If a hungry fish fears for its life it will decide to delay feeding until the danger has passed or it will move to an area where it can feed in safety.

Fish feeding on the same food may influence barbel behaviour in two ways. Firstly, they may attract the barbel to the food source and secondly, they compete for the food by consuming it or preventing the barbel from consuming it. My observations suggest that barbel are definitely attracted by other fish feeding and they have the bulk to remove other competitors like chub. Large barbel seem to be able to displace smaller barbel from productive feeding sites.

Barbel searching or foraging for food detect it using sight and smell but will not ingest it until they have tasted and touched it. Much research has been conducted into the identification of feeding stimulants and food selection in fish. One important factor has emerged and that is that chemicals which stimulate fish to feed are not necessarily the ones that humans can detect with their noses. This is because the sense of smell in water depends on the solubility of chemicals and not on their volatility.

For the scientists reading this, the work so far has demonstrated that stimulants seem specific to species, to be of low molecular weight, are non-volatile, nitrogenous and amphoteric. Amino acids fall into this group but as far as I know, no work has been done on *Barbus barbus*. Food abundance also influences feeding behaviour and if large quantities of one food type are available, fish may feed exclusively on it, ignoring other items. Such fish are said to have developed a specific search image. Food abundance will also stimulate a resting fish to engage in feeding.

Fish behaviour can be modified by experience. They can learn which areas of a river are productive for food and experiments have shown that fish can learn to recognise new foods and avoid ones that will harm them. This has very obvious implications for anglers and will be discussed later in this chapter.

Influence of River Conditions on Feeding

In my experience, the three main physico/chemical factors that may influence the barbel's feeding behaviour are temperature, current velocity and light intensity. There are other environmental variables that have the potential to influence barbel, for example pH and oxygen concentration, but I rarely find that they influence barbel behaviour in relation to fishing. Very occasionally, a long hot dry spell will result in low oxygen concentrations and the barbel will then move into or below shallow broken water which is normally well oxygenated.

Fish are described as being 'cold-blooded' or, more properly, poikilothermic. This means that they have no mechanism for maintaining a constant internal body temperature and so it varies with that of their environment. All poikilotherms function best within a certain temperature range and when the temperature of their environment falls below or rises above this range the animals cease to feed and the temperature is said to be limiting. I cannot find any experimental evidence on the preferred temperature range of barbel but in my angling experience I have yet to record an upper or lower limit to their feeding. I have caught barbel when the river temperature has been as high as 20°C and as low as 3°C. Having said this, on some rivers I have never caught them when the river temperature has been below 6°C and so I believe that there is probably variability between populations in the various rivers in which I have fished.

All temperatures are relative, however, and so in winter a reading of 7°C after a cold spell of 4°C is more promising than after a mild spell of 10°C. Similarly, if cold weather has prevailed for a considerable period then barbel may start to feed out of sheer hunger. Warm water does not seem to put barbel off the feed at all but as already mentioned it may affect their distribution by influencing the dissolved oxygen concentration.

In Europe, barbel are known to hibernate by packing together in sheltered areas of water. This was shown in a wonderful underwater film made by Hans Siegel of Germany. He found shoals of barbel packed, side by side, in hollows within undercut banks. They may also do this in England but I have never seen it during my winter diving expeditions. I have, however, caught a great many more barbel during mild winter spells than during cold periods and there is absolutely no doubt in my mind that temperature has a major influence on barbel feeding behaviour.

Current velocity has a direct and indirect effect on barbel. Although they seem to live in relatively fast stretches of river they often seek sheltered refuges. During times of elevated flow barbel will often be found in bankside slacks and areas of quiet water. This may not restrict their feeding behaviour, in fact it may do just the opposite because there is scientific data to demonstrate that during elevated or flood conditions the numbers of aquatic and terrestrial invertebrates carried in the current is greatly increased. Certainly, barbel feed very well during these conditions and this may be in response to the increased food availability.

Lastly, light seems to affect the location of barbel. Most seem to shun bright light by hiding under weed or seeking deep water. This may be because they feel vulnerable to predation in such conditions. Most certainly when the river is coloured by sediment, or when the sun dips below the horizon, barbel are found in open, shallow runs that they would not usually occupy during clearly lit conditions.

USING THIS INFORMATION TO CATCH BARBEL

Do Not be Seen as a Predator

Successful angling depends on the correct timing of trips, location of fish and use of techniques and baits. Essentially, the angler must use a bait that barbel will recognise as food, present that bait where the fish are located

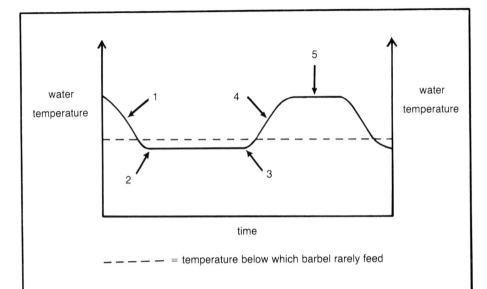

_ _ _ _ _ = temperature below which barbel rarely feed

1 – Temperature falling – fish probably not feeding.

2 – Temperature has fallen below 'feeding limit' – fish almost certainly not feeding.

3 – Water temperature has been below 'feeding limit' for several days – barbel may begin to feed because of hunger.

4 and 5 – Temperature rising and steady, well above limiting level – barbel probably feeding.

The influence of temperature on feeding.

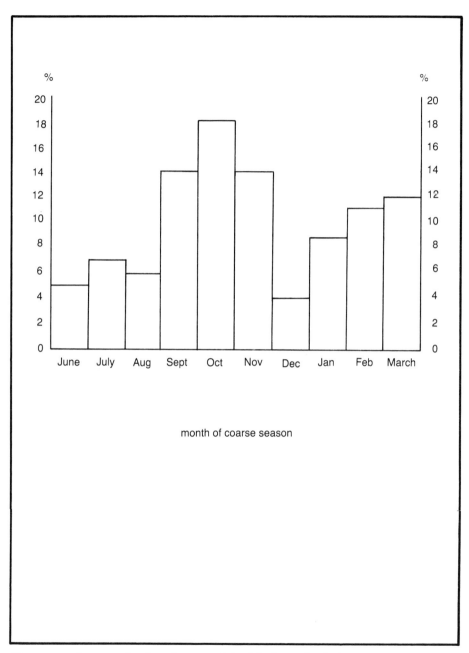

Histogram showing the distribution of double-figure barbel reported to the angling press during the 1987–8 and 1988–9 seasons. Low temperature is probably the cause of the few captures in December.

and do everything he can not to scare or spook his quarry so that it will not refuse to take his offering.

We have seen that the fear of predation will prevent a barbel from feeding. Anglers should regard themselves as predators because their movements on the bank may signal danger to the fish. Stealth and concealment are most important so standing upright on the river bank, shouting and dropping heavy tackle on the ground is ill advised. The way some fishermen stomp about on the bank and yell to their mates still amazes me. I am certain that they would catch so many more fish if they adopted a more stealthy approach.

There is no doubt that fish can learn and they can become bait- and tackle-shy. I have seen barbel bolt in terror at the sight of a cube of luncheon meat and also at the sight of a swim feeder. This behaviour is most common when they are exposed on gravel runs because I have seen exactly the same fish tolerate the presence of these items when they are holed up under weed. If you are not catching barbel it may be because you have spooked them with a bait that they have been caught on before or with terminal tackle which they associate with danger. A change may result in fish on the bank. Alternatively, if you can actually present your bait in a place where barbel feel secure you may get a take when the same bait has been ignored out in the open.

The Best Conditions for Fishing

Barbel fishermen can also influence their chances of success by choosing the best occasions to be on the bank. Barbel are least likely to feed when there has been a sudden drop in water temperature or if it is below a limiting temperature which varies from river to river. I honestly believe that there is little point in fishing for them in these situations and so I go after other fish like chub. Low river temperatures will also depress their body temperatures and therefore their rate of metabolism. The process of digestion will take longer and so they will feel hungry less often.

The conditions when they feed best are after heavy rain when the river is coloured with sediment and is carrying more food items, and when light intensities are low, either at night or in dull overcast weather. In winter a coloured river often follows warm weather. The river temperature will be raised by a few degrees and this may also stimulate the barbel to feed. For example, on the Hampshire Avon a cold winter river temperature is about 4°C but after warm rain it can go up to 8, 9, or even 10°C. Whenever this happens I make sure I have got a bait in a hot barbel swim.

Lock into Those Feeding Rhythms

Physical conditions in rivers display rhythmical changes or periodicity. Water temperatures fluctuate seasonally and light intensity varies daily. It is no surprise, therefore, that fish behaviour is also rhythmical. The most striking example, and possibly the most relevant, is that of daily feeding times. Barbel that have sought shelter during the daylight hours will emerge in the evening and start feeding.

Feeding rhythms definitely vary from river to river and from stretch to stretch. Anglers influence them enormously by introducing quantities of bait. I remember one swim on Throop Fishery always producing a fish at 6.15 p.m., while another spot produced one at noon!

As a general rule, I think that, during daylight, you will have to work harder and introduce more feed than in the evening or at night.

Stimulating Barbel to Feed

Anglers stimulate fish to feed with groundbait and loose feed. Barbel holed up under weed in bright sunny conditions can be lured out on to gravel runs

Even in the low evening light it is important to avoid being spotted by the barbel.

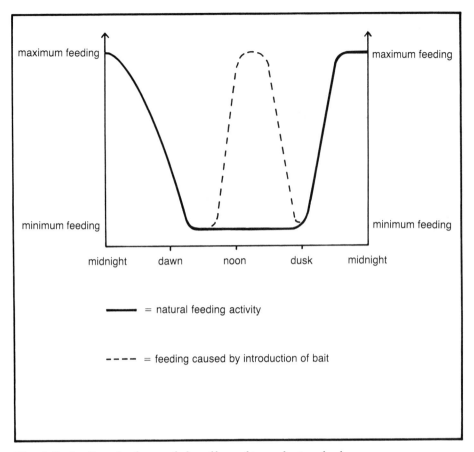

The daily feeding rhythm and the effect of introducing feed.

and made to start eating. Particle baits seem best for this and I think it may be because the presence of masses of tiny food items imitates natural phenomena like a hatch of insects. I am sure that in this situation the barbel are stimulated, visually, by a plethora of food.

Never underestimate the importance of feed. On countless occasions I have watched barbel sheltering under cover but have coaxed them out with bait. It is fascinating to watch them become more and more agitated as you introduce more and more food. Suddenly, one fish will dart from the sanctuary and then others will follow. When they really start feeding in earnest they charge about and dig ferociously into the bottom, often moving quite large rocks with their snouts.

The sense of smell is important to barbel when they are searching for food. You can help them find your bait when they are foraging by using

Keeping low to avoid scaring the fish.

groundbait and loose feed to increase the concentration of dissolved chemicals being wafted downstream by the river's currents. When they find your hookbait they will test it by feeling it with their barbules and tasting it with their mouths. I have also watched barbel creep up upon a hookbait from downstream and then sit and study it visually for up to fifteen minutes before either taking it or swimming away. Bait presentation can, therefore, make all the difference between getting and not getting any bites. There is little doubt that barbel are often interested in feeding on baits but detect something which makes fear and self-preservation override their hunger.

Although there is some scientific evidence to demonstrate the importance of amino acids as feeding stimulants, it must be said that this area of fish biology is in its infancy. I strongly suggest that your time would be better spent on other aspects of barbel angling rather than delving into the world of chemicals. Barbel take a great variety of baits and eat a number of different foods in the wild. This suggests that they respond to a wide range of chemical stimulants which are already present in the baits available to you. If you are still determined to waft amino acids down to your local barbel population then I suggest you use fish meal. This stuff fairly oozes with aminos.

Do Not Overfeed or Underfeed Them

One of the most difficult decisions for any angler is how much feed to use. If you use too little you may not get the fish interested and if you use too much you will fill them up and they will cease eating.

Large shoals of barbel, and those in the River Severn are a good example, can consume huge quantities of feed whereas one solitary specimen in the Dorset Stour obviously would not. There can be no hard-and-fast rules about a feeding strategy and you must weigh up each situation as it arises.

Novel Baits and Prebaiting

Although barbel can learn about new foods, they seem to take much longer than other species to do so. Carp or chub, for example, will inspect a new food item and will often take it. The phrase 'curiosity feeding' has been coined to describe this behaviour. I do not think barbel are very curious and I know of several anglers who have introduced large quantities of a bait into a stretch of water and never got barbel to take it.

Unless you can conduct a very heavy and regular prebaiting campaign, it may be a better strategy to stick to conventional baits which barbel have learned to take, and to concentrate on presenting them properly.

I very much hope that this chapter has stimulated you to seek more information about fish and freshwater biology. Knowledge will help you to fish more effectively even if, like me, you can sometimes only make an educated guess about what to do. One thing is certain and that is that there is a very big difference between an educated guess and a wild one.

Fish Location and Rivercraft

The pleasure derived from sitting by a lovely river is enormous. Flowing water has a magnetic attraction and it is possible to sit for hours watching the gentle sway of weed and listening to the quiet rustle of rushes. To catch a barbel is almost a bonus.

Any river owes its character to the current and bedrock over which it flows. With the passing of each season the riverine moods change – at one extreme, a swollen and freezing aggressor tearing at the banks; at the other, the low clear waters of summer skimmed by damselflies and swallows. This dynamism produces perpetual change. The processes of erosion and deposi-

The Hampshire Avon is a river whose nature is affected by the chalk downs from which it rises.

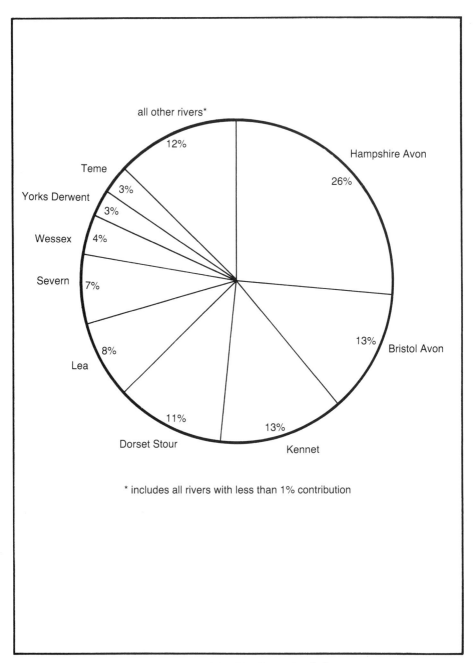

Pie chart showing the percentage of double-figure barbel caught from different rivers and reported to the angling press during the 1987–8 and 1988–9 seasons.

tion are relentless and no fishery will ever be exactly as it was the previous year.

Each river displays a huge variety of habitats both along its length and across its width. This spatial variety causes fish populations to display clumped distributions. Instead of being spread out at random they will only live in those parts of the river that suit them. The main factors that influence the location of river fish are current velocity, type of bottom or substrate, depth of water and the presence of cover such as weed or overhanging trees. Food availability, the presence of predators, light intensity and temperature will also have an effect.

Fish location will also vary on a daily and seasonal basis. At night, for example, barbel will venture into shallow water and in the winter, when weed cover is scarce, they will be found in other areas of shelter.

For an angler to locate his quarry reliably, he must often look at the surface of a river and try to visualise what is happening underneath it. This chapter discusses the habitat preferences of barbel and the methods used by anglers to find these holding areas and so locate their quarry.

Observing barbel on the Severn.

WHICH RIVER AND FISHERY TO CHOOSE

The logical sequence when deciding where to fish for barbel is river, fishery, swim and precise area of swim. When you select a river you must decide whether you want quantity or quality of fish. Some rivers like the Teme and Severn abound with small- to medium-size barbel but if you want a double then it would be wise to get into the car and travel to specific stretches of rivers like the Dorset Stour or Hampshire Avon.

Sources of information on barbel populations abound. The two weekly angling papers are very useful and so are angling books and magazines. Many people will be willing to assist you and tackle dealers, fishing club secretaries and the 'grape-vine' will all help.

Different fisheries within one river vary enormously in their numbers and average size of barbel. The Hampshire Avon provides a good example of this when one compares a stretch like the Severals below Ringwood with the area between Fordingbridge and Salisbury. The former has quite a head of barbel and the latter nowhere near as many. The average size on one

Using a notebook to record the nature of this area during low-water.

*Taking the water temperature with a modern digital
thermometer.*

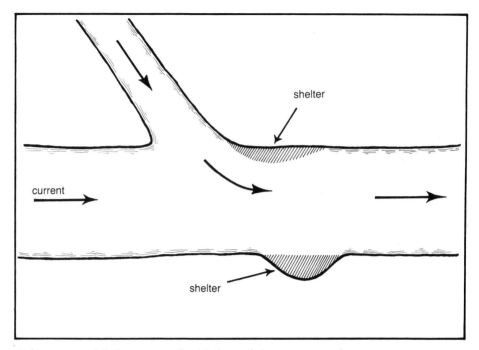

Other areas of shelter are cattle drinks and downstream of tributaries.

water near Breamore is 7–8lb whereas on the Severals it is below this, although there are still some very big fish to be taken there.

Such information offers two extremes. You can try to ignore all advice and information from other people or you can follow a successful angler, wait for him to vacate his swim and then stick your bait exactly where he put his. Personally, I derive a great deal of pleasure from trying to pioneer new stretches and swims but I will not pretend for one minute that I have not received help from other people on many occasions.

If you too have the pioneering spirit and want to fish a water that is not known to contain barbel there are some signs to look for. I think that stretches with medium flow over clean gravel bottoms, with a variety of depths and plenty of weed like ranunculus to provide shelter, are ideal. For winter barbelling add in some deep slacks and eddies and you will have a water with potential.

Maps can be tremendously useful. I use the Ordnance Survey Pathfinder Series which have a scale of 1:25,000. These show just enough detail so that

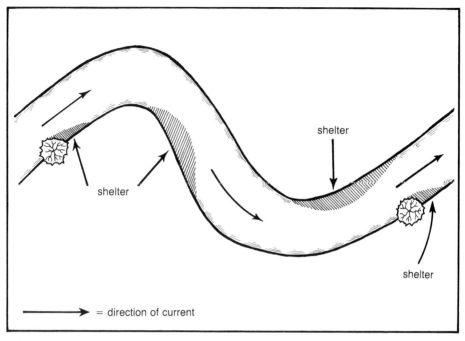

When constructing a map, note areas of sheltered water on the inside of bends and behind overhanging trees.

I can identify the larger river features like islands, sharp bends and narrow and broad widths.

DIRECTLY AND INDIRECTLY OBSERVING BARBEL

Guesswork about barbel location and size can be eliminated if you can actually see them. Unfortunately, this is often impossible because of deep water, dense weed or coloured conditions.

Where waters are clear and shallow spend as much time as you can on the bank, leaning over bridges and gazing from trees. If it is permitted, you may be able to see them when drifting down the river current in a canoe. A decent pair of polarising sunglasses are a must for this type of observation and a small pair of binoculars will also be helpful. Early morning and evening are good times to see barbel and in late May or early June you may be treated to a glimpse of them spawning.

Alternatively, you can scan the shallows at night with a powerful torch but make sure that you do not antagonise any other anglers. You may hear barbel 'clooping' at night. This occurs when they turn upside-down and suck food items from surface weed. Other fish, like chub, also do this and so you must verify that clooping fish are barbel, with a torch.

Barbel also roll on the surface and they often do this during floods. Again, other species roll and you really must be close to them to make absolutely sure of identification.

The best indirect evidence of the presence of barbel is left after they have been feeding in shallow water. Gravel shallows develop a covering of green algae when exposed to sunlight. When barbel have been grubbing around, they leave clean areas which look as though they have been hoovered. The size of these varies from dinner-plate size to dustbin-lid size and there may be several on one stretch of shallows.

There remains one last and very specialised method of observing barbel and that is by subaqua diving. Do not even contemplate this if you are not a fully trained scuba diver and cannot dive with a companion or 'buddy'. River currents are dangerous and so is diving equipment if you do not know how to use it.

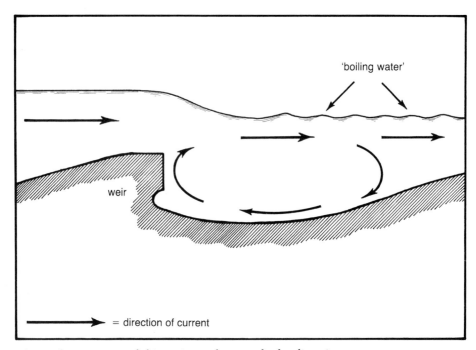

The surface current of this weir pool conceals the direction of flow over the weir bed.

MAPPING THE WATER

Once you have decided which water to fish it is necessary to get to know it like the back of your hand. You must understand where the barbel are likely to be during any type of conditions that you encounter on a fishing trip. It is at this stage that you must construct your own map of the river, even if it is just a mental one on the day you turn up to fish. The most important features to include on it are depth of water, current, type of bottom and areas of shelter like weed beds and deep holes. If you are analysing these when the river is low you must try to imagine how the river will change when it is in flood and store this information for future use.

Mapping weed beds is easy. Plumbing the depth is not too hard either but it needs to be done very carefully or you may miss some vital fish-holding feature like a sudden depression in the river bed. A shallow gravel run can suddenly drop into a deeper hole of just a yard or so in length. This is just the sort of spot where barbel lie to escape the main force of the current. Clumsy plumbing may miss such an area.

Investigating the river current is very difficult from the bank because what you see on the surface is often very different from what is occurring on the bottom. The surface water will almost always be the fastest but directly beneath it the currents may be almost still. The surface current does provide some clues. If it is smooth with little sign of turbulence it is likely that the bottom is also relatively level. Any 'boils' on the surface will, however, be produced by a feature of some kind like a sunken log, large rock or hidden weed bed. Any such bottom feature will influence the current behind it and may produce an area of sheltered water where barbel are likely to lie.

Currents tolerated by barbel will vary. If they are hungry and find a valuable source of food they will enter a fast run because the energy to be gained from the food will be greater than that required to get it. If they are not hungry, either through being full or because they will not feed in a low water temperature, they will avoid fast currents and will seek sheltered areas.

The difference between what an angler sees on the surface and what is happening on the river bed was brought home to me when I donned an aqualung and plunged into a River Kennet weir pool. The surface was a raging torrent but underneath the weir race the water was almost motionless. I could swim about with ease! Even in a uniform run the current will always be slowest at the river bed because of the friction exerted by gravel and weed, a vital point to remember when you are trotting a bait.

Trying to decide where the fish will be.

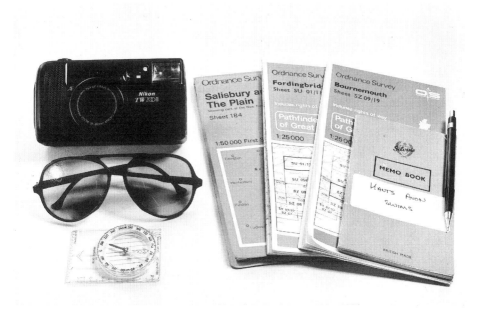

Equipment needed to find and record potential barbel swims: camera, polaroids, compass, maps and notebook.

The river bottom will also provide indirect evidence as to the current velocity on the river bed. The faster the current, the larger the particle size on the bottom. For example, at a speed of 300cm a second the current will move boulders about the size of a human head; at half that speed it will move small stones and at 25cm a second it will move sand. Therefore, if you find a sandy spot it suggests that it is a sheltered one which rarely, if ever, gets exposed to fast currents.

To analyse the river bed, stick a heavyish leger of about 1½oz on a strong line and cast it all over the river. When you drag it back across the bottom, the vibrations that you feel are related to the particle size of the river bed. Jagged, irregular vibrations indicate stones or coarse gravel and small, regular vibrations indicate relatively fine gravel. A soggy unyielding pull means weed!

Bank features like cattle drinks or a tree with large projecting roots can be noted and it is often worth taking a photograph. The benefit of this will be apparent when you turn up and find the river carrying an extra six feet of impenetrably murky water! If you know that one cattle drink has a lovely clean gravel bottom and that another one has an old motorbike and a bed of nettles in it you may well choose the former for yourself and stick your mate in the other one.

Lastly, but very importantly, I note any aspect of individual swims that will affect my fishing. For example, trees may inhibit me playing a big fish and some swims are very exposed. I record which direction swims face with a small compass, then, whenever there is a force 8 gale blowing I know which swims will be most comfortable to fish according to the direction of the wind. This is vital because sometimes the very best river conditions coincide with atrocious weather. Westerly gales often blow in lovely warm rain and if you know that one swim faces west and another faces east then the latter will be much more comfortable to fish in.

In recent years, modern electronic depth sounders have been used by anglers both to analyse depths and directly locate fish. They may be necessary on a huge lake but I do not think that they are needed or desirable on British rivers. If you are capable of finding fish without them you will be a better angler for it. Having said that, some Thames weir pools, for example, could only be surveyed with a sounder. So, although I have a personal dislike for such equipment on rivers it may well have a place on the larger ones.

Low-river in the summer.

The same shot during a winter flood – if you had the first picture to refer to you could make a better decision about where to fish.

LOCATING THE BARBEL

Once you have a good picture of the physical characteristics of a river, certain swims will positively scream barbel at you. Certain combinations of current, depth, bottom and cover will look great.

In the summer and autumn, during daylight, most barbel will seek shelter. For every one out on an exposed gravel run I estimate that there will be a dozen sheltering under weed, an overhanging bank or other feature. If you cannot see them, then you will just have to start fishing for them. It is the only way. The best locations seem to be clean gravel under or behind shelter and the gravel size will often be smaller than on the exposed runs suggesting quieter areas of current. The depth of these swims is unlikely to be below three feet but this will vary from fishery to fishery and also during a season. Productive early summer swims are often fast and weedy. This has been attributed to the fish 'cleaning themselves' after spawning but I am not sure what interpretation to put on it.

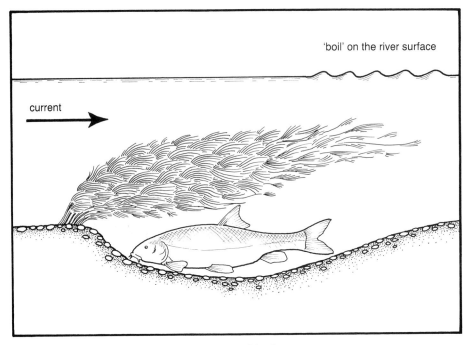

Barbel sheltering in a hollow below a weed bed.

At night, barbel are less cautious and will venture from their daytime homes and scour exposed gravel runs for food. During darkness, depth of water becomes much less important and the fish can be found in shallows of eighteen inches or even less.

If you cannot see the fish, or any evidence of their presence, location is more difficult when rivers are low or at normal level because often the number of good-looking swims outnumbers the number of barbel in the fishery. You just have to fish as long and as often as you can to identify which areas they frequent most. Alternatively, sit tight and feed a swim in the hope that the fish will be drawn towards you. A good strategy on an unfamiliar water is to adopt a roving approach for the first few sessions and spend ten minutes in as many different swims as possible. This way you will get to know a fishery very quickly and good swims will not remain undiscovered because you were concentrating elsewhere.

When rivers are high and the flood currents are strong, barbel location is simpler because they seek quiet areas of the river where they can shelter from the current. Bank-side slacks and eddies and depressions in the river bed are the places to find them and sometimes the entire population of a stretch will be packed into a relatively small area.

In winter, barbel haunts will be different from those of the summer. This is hardly surprising because in winter virtually all the weed has gone, the water is more coloured and the currents are stronger. Temperature also exerts an important influence in winter. Barbel shelter from currents to save energy. The faster the current and the lower the temperature of the water, the more energy a barbel will have to use in order to maintain position. Water near 0°C is about 70 per cent more viscous than water at 20°C so you can see why in cold winter rivers barbel are even more keen to avoid harsh currents. Deep slacks and hollows are the places to find them, especially during strong floods.

An important point to make about river temperatures is that, unlike lakes, they show very little stratification. The river current is constantly being mixed and so the temperature at the edge is likely to be exactly the same as it is in the middle. As long as you stick your thermometer in a flowing area and not in a frozen puddle you will record the temperature being experienced by your quarry.

Winter swims are often difficult to find because some look good but never produce fish. It is worth putting a lot of effort into finding them, however, because I have found that such swims can produce fish winter after winter.

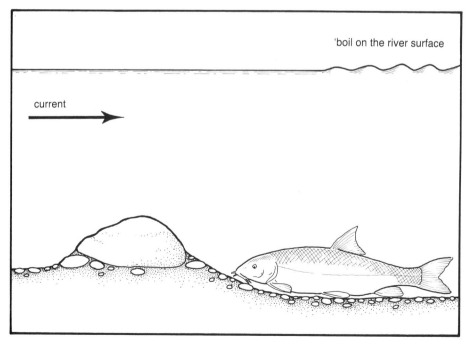

Barbel sheltering behind a rise in the river bed.

Barbel love to hide under overhanging banks.

LOCATING THE BIGGEST BARBEL

If you want 10lb barbel or fish even bigger than that, you must put even more time and effort into locating them. You may be lucky enough to see them but if you cannot, where do you start?

I believe that it is impossible to look at a particular water and say, 'that will produce doubles'. Big barbel have been captured from the most unlikely looking places but, in general, I would advise looking for plenty of cover, moderate pace of current and good average depth.

The angling press, the grape-vine, local reports and tackle dealers are probably your best bet for information on big fish. Water authorities are also helpful and their fishery biologists sometimes have scale readings and growth estimates for different populations.

Data gathered from two seasons of reports to the angling press suggest that the vast majority of doubles are taken from southern rivers. The Hampshire Avon, Bristol Avon, Kennet and Dorset Stour produce the most, so if you are hell-bent on a double then it is worth travelling to get them.

58

SUMMARY

Time spent on reconnaissance is never wasted. The better you know your water, the better you will be able to respond to the variety of conditions that you will inevitably encounter over a fishing season. The best example I can give is one particular Middle Avon fishery. The first year I fished it I caught a solitary barbel, the second, I had about a dozen and in the third, when I knew the water like the back of my hand, I had over fifty. When I drove to that stretch, I knew I would catch.

Tackle

CHOOSING YOUR LINE

I regard two items of tackle as the most important for barbel fishing. The first is line because without a strong, reliable brand on your reel you might as well not start after barbel at all. The power combination of a muscular barbel exploiting a fast river current is tremendous and it will stretch your gear to the limit.

Choosing a line is a matter of compromise because it should be very strong, very thin, extremely limp and supple, resistant to abrasion and have

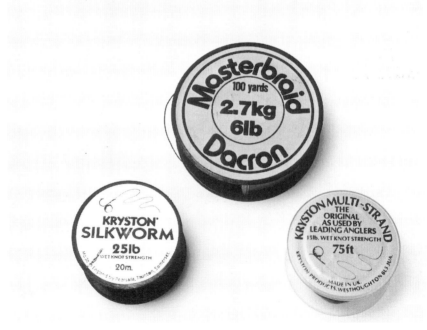

Modern trace lines to use if your barbel are spooked by ordinary mono.

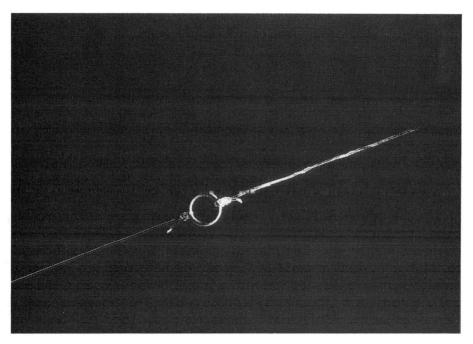

*Mono is easily damaged and can be checked by holding up
against the light.*

a high wet knot strength. Unfortunately, none exists which combines all of
these features.

After many seasons I have settled for Maxima as the main line loaded on
my reels. This line is quite manageable, very reliable and of reasonable
diameter. It is, however, fragile and a bulk spool only lasts a season.
Manageability is important, particularly at night, and a line which keeps
twisting up and springing off your reels can lead to disaster as well as being
infuriating.

Eight-pound BS is my main leger line and 4lb my main float line. Maxima
needs regular greasing for trotting because it is quite a heavy line. Occasionally, 10lb or even 12lb line is needed for very snaggy swims where you 'hit,
hold and haul' and, conversely, on rivers with little weed and no snags I
reduce the reel line to 6lb. This is because the thinner the line I can get away
with using, the lighter the legers I need to hold a bait in position.

A different brand is called for when a thinner trace is required and this is
where Drennan Double Strength scores. This is a very thin line for its
strength. For example, 6lb BS Maxima is 0.22mm in diameter and 10lb BS
Double Strength is only 0.23mm in diameter. However, this type of line is

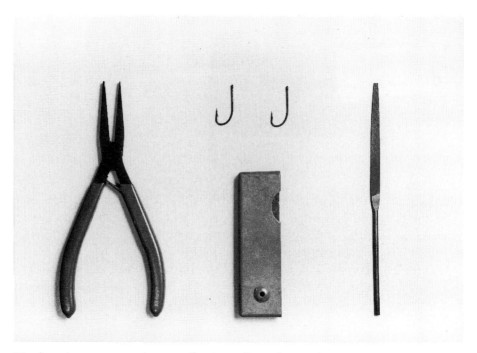

Hook maintenance equipment: flat-jaw pliers, sharpening stone and small file.

extremely intolerant of abuse. Kinks and bad knots reduce its strength dramatically and so all traces must be inspected and tested regularly. This disadvantage is outweighed, in my opinion, when a thin but strong trace overcomes a wary, tackle-shy fish. I keep a range from 10lb BS down to 4lb BS and it has caught me some fine barbel that would not take a bait presented on 8lb Maxima.

If I cannot get takes, even on Double Strength, I keep two types of trace material in my bag – Masterbraid Dacron and Kryston Multistrand. Both of these are more supple and soft than ordinary mono. I am very impressed with the softness of the Multistrand when in water. When it separates into its many different fibres it is also impossible to detect.

Good line is vital and is one of the best investments any barbel angler can make. Spending time on decent knots is another. The grinner is superb and, when tied properly, never comes undone. It is the most reliable knot I have used in over thirty years of angling, however, four turns are needed for Multistrand instead of the normal three. The double grinner is good for joining two lengths of line but tests have shown me that it is not as strong as using two single grinners and a swivel or Drennan ring. Every single knot I tie is tested with a strong and steady pull of several pounds. This is because every now and again a grinner will weaken the line. For example, it can reduce 8lb BS Maxima to a strength of about 1lb BS! The time to discover that is definitely before casting out because it is sheer agony to put a tremendous amount of effort into a session only to get broken on the strike.

HOOKS

Hooks are the second of the two most important items of tackle. Together with the line, and protected by a good rod, reel and playing technique, a decent hook will land you your barbel. If you try to save money by buying cheap ones you are crazy.

Luckily for barbel anglers, the tackle manufacturers have produced some excellent varieties. I need two types: big strong, heavy ones for medium to large baits and smaller lighter ones for presenting baits like maggots.

I have used several of the big strong variety and can wholeheartedly recommend Au Lion D'Or, series 1534, Drennan Super Specialist, Sprite Carp Hooks and the Partridge Specialist Carp hooks. These all mean business and are made by very reputable firms. However, every now and again a dud creeps through the quality control procedures of the

The sort of duff hook to look out for.

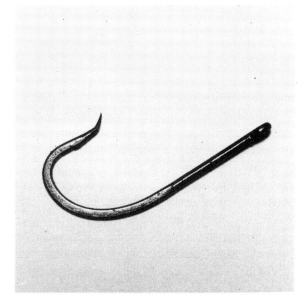

manufacturers so it is best to check every one for faults. This can be done with a close visual inspection and then by holding the hook by the shank in some forceps and giving it a strong tweak with your index finger. Very rarely, but often enough to make it worthwhile, a brittle hook snaps or a soft one bends. It is best to discover such things before you latch into a big barbel.

Ideally, for small light baits a fine wire hook is needed for decent presentation. Unfortunately, hooking a decent barbel on a fine wire hook is a bit like tethering a raging bull with a length of cotton. I compromise and use medium wire hooks and recently I have had very good results with Drennan Specialist Crystals. A range of sizes which include 2 to 12, for the strong hooks, and 8 to 14, for the lighter ones, caters for most situations.

To barb or not to barb? I do not, but I buy barbed hooks and squeeze the barbs down to leave a small bump. The advantages of these modified hooks over the barbed originals are that they penetrate more easily and speed up hook removal from a barbel on the bank. The theoretical disadvantage is that they may fall out of a hooked fish but this has never happened to me in many years of barbel fishing.

Good hooks require good care and so it is worth keeping a small hook sharpener and pair of flat-jaw pliers in your kit. Keep your hooks needle sharp, test and inspect them regularly and they will not let you down.

The hook on the right has had the barb squeezed flat. This aids hook penetration on the strike and unhooking.

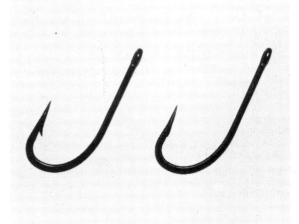

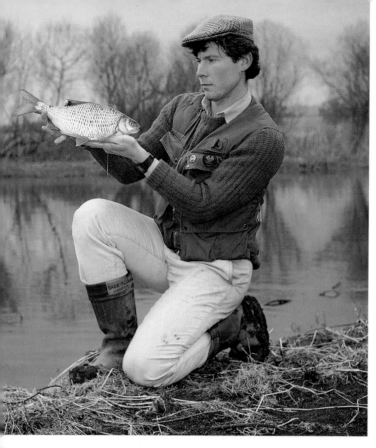

A big roach caught trotting
bread in the Hampshire
Avon. In the evening I
changed to leger tactics and
caught barbel.

Carefully returning a big
double-figure barbel.

A close up of a large barbel. The depth of its belly shows what good condition it was in.

Opposite: *A big winter fish.*

A near double from the Avon which is slightly deformed. I've caught it twice in swims about a mile apart.

A period after big chub like this one can often be fitted into a barbel session.

I've caught barbel and pike from the same swims in winter.

Returning a lovely barbel.

How's this for determination – myself on an investigative diving session in January!

This barbel is sheltering from the river current under a rock.

*A major motivating force for me is the need to be in
beautiful places.*

A flooded river in winter — my favourite conditions.

Overleaf: *Waiting for a barbel take at dusk.*

A sunken log is protecting this barbel from the river bank and would be a formidable snag!

RODS

Barbel live in various types of river and there are many different ways of catching them. No one rod can cope with this variety and to ask a barbel angler to stick to one rod is like asking a golfer to play a round with just a putter.

I have now narrowed my range of barbel rods to just five but before I describe them let us consider the various functions that a rod must perform: casting or controlling a bait to the barbel, indicating the bite on the tip (in the case of leger rods), picking up line and setting the hook when striking, and protecting the line and hook-hold during the fight. The characteristics of a good rod are lightness with strength, slim diameter and 'feel'

If a rod is going to be held throughout a long session then a light one is obviously best. A slim one comes into its own during strong winds. The slimmer it is, the less it will be buffeted by gusts and the less likely you are to miss bites or lose control of your float. 'Feel' really means the transmission of information to the angler. This could be about the pull of a float, the fight or bite of a fish or the nature of the river bed as a leger rolls over it or gets stuck in weed. A soggy old flop pole will not tell you much at all.

All in all, I think that carbon is the best material for all of these functions. The one advantage that glass rods or some cane rods have is that they may be more forgiving when playing a fish. My rods include: a trotting rod for trundling a bait down a gravel run – a 12ft Daiwa 'Ivan Marks Harrier' which is nicely balanced with a 3-lb line. It has plenty of action in the middle section for soaking up the fight but is occasionally a bit short for proper float control. A longer rod would be better but would be hell to play a barbel on. I once caught a nine pounder on a 13-ft tip-action match rod and my arm ached for ages afterwards. I don't think that the barbel appreciated the forty-minute fight either.

Secondly, I have a short-range leger rod. This is the one that I use for most of my barbelling. It has a 10-foot 1lb test curve, all-through or slow-action Tricast, carbon/kevlar blank, and the tip ring is threaded for a quiver should the need arise. (By short range I mean any swim that can be cast to under-arm.) It can handle leads up to $1^{1}/_{2}$oz and, in combination with 8lb BS Maxima and a good hook, I have yet to find a barbel that can beat it. This rod is strong, light and a joy to fish with, especially when roving from swim to swim.

Thirdly, I have a medium range leger rod for situations that the ten-footer cannot cope with. For example, chucking a medium feeder some distance into a swollen River Severn. This one has an 11-foot 1¼lb test curve Masterline carbon blank. Its action is slightly faster than 'all through' and the stiffer butt means that I have to be more careful when playing a fish to the net. This rod has a built-in quiver and I often fish a pair. It can also be used at short range when I have to shift a heavy feeder when striking a hook into a fish.

On occasion, the need arises to fish at some range in a river and/or keep as much line off the current as possible. Here, a powerful twelve footer comes into its own and the best I have used so far is Drennan's Heavy Feeder.

Lastly, my 'Stick' is for getting into tangles of overhanging, bank-side vegetation and lowering a bait towards fish living underneath. It is 7ft long, has a test curve of about 1½lb and a glass blank of unknown origin.

Many successful barbel anglers use rods very different to these. It is purely a matter of personal choice but all have one thing in common – the blank is balanced to the line strength. Nothing will lose you your barbel more quickly than fishing with a rod that is too strong for your line. A traditional guide is to multiply your rod's test curve by four to get the correct combination. However, I think that is a bit on the strong side and would suggest multiplying by five or six. For playing barbel, all-through action blanks are superior to fast taper ones because they soak up the barbel's lunges in a more progressive fashion and, therefore, protect the line and hook-hold better. I really see little need for fast taper rods in barbel fishing, unless you are going to fish at considerable range in a large river, because their main benefit is the ability to set hooks at distance and that is very rarely necessary in barbel angling.

Where I differ from some anglers is that I do not always use a built-in quiver on my barbel leger rods. The reasons for this will be discussed in the section on touch legering.

Whatever rods you choose to fish for barbel with, the more you use them, the more they become an extension of your arm and will be 'second nature' to use.

Rod Supports

I need two types of rod support: one type for when I touch leger and hold the rod and another type for when I fish two rods in parallel and watch the tops or quivers for bites.

For touch legering when bites are slow in coming it is worth using one rod rest to take some of the weight of the rod and reel. A support also helps to steady the rod in windy conditions and so helps in bite detection. Simple designs that do not trap line are needed so that tugs, twitches and tweaks are transmitted to my fingers.

For fishing two rods I use buzzer bars which have been wrapped in cloth. The cloth protects the varnish on the rod and stops the rods sliding on the bar (*see* photograph, page 99). This arrangement allows me to position the rods so that the butts are about a foot apart and the tips are almost touching.

Good bank sticks to attach these supports to are made by several manu-facturers. They are a good investment and last years.

REELS

Reels for barbel fishing have a relatively simple job to do. They must release line for mostly short casting distances, when you want to trot a float and when you need to let a fighting fish run. Then they must recover it. The quality that they must possess is reliability. A good reel will do all these tasks trip after trip and season after season, and with a minimum of maintenance.

I have caught barbel on centrepins but prefer fixed spool
reels in case I need to regain line rapidly.

This sort of coarse mesh landing net should be avoided for barbel because they damage the fins and scales.

I use a Mitchell Match 440 for legering and a Leeds centrepin for trotting. The Mitchell has proved itself to be tough and reliable. The feature I like on this model is the locking bale arm which is essential for touch legering. This is because the line from my fingers does not always lie under the bale arm roller and the sudden pressure of striking can open an unlocked bale arm resulting in line being released and the fish being lost. Where the Mitchell can let me down is when it allows the line to get behind the spool. However, I always regard this as my fault for not checking for it.

There are a great many excellent fixed-spool reels available that are made by other manufacturers. Two major advantages of many over the Mitchell Match are skirted spools and price. The Ryobi GR2 has proved itself to be a delightful little reel to balance a carbon leger rod and I find that I am using it with increasing frequency.

The Leeds centrepin is a great trotting reel and allows much steadier control of a float than the fixed-spool Mitchell. That, I believe, is its only advantage as casting is easier with the Mitchell and playing a fish is safer because the faster retrieve permits me to keep up with a hooked fish that suddenly runs towards me. With a centrepin, this may result in slack line which I daren't allow with my barbless hooks. Again, this is only my personal preference and other anglers swear by centrepins and catch a great many big barbel with them.

LANDING NETS

Very big barbel are 30in and over in length so a landing net with 36in arms is about right. River banks vary enormously in height and marginal weed can extend out quite a distance. It is best to have a pole that extends from 4–7ft so that you can reach out to a beaten fish.

Controversy has raged in the past about the type of mesh to use in landing nets – micro or coarse? Those for coarse mesh say that micro mesh nets get caught in river currents and make landing fish very difficult. Those for micro mesh nets say that landing the barbel is a bit more difficult but coarse mesh nets damage the fish. I am in the latter group because fish care is my priority and there is no doubt at all that coarse mesh nets can damage a barbel's dorsal fin.

LEGERS AND FEEDERS

A good leger will: enter the river without too much noise, either anchor the bait firmly in position or roll in a controlled fashion to the position that you want, not get caught up in weed, debris or snags, not scare the fish visually, and not impede the strike and prevent hook penetration. In addition to these functions, a feeder will deliver hook samples or groundbait.

Three physical factors influence the performance of a leger: weight, shape and colour. In British barbel rivers, a range of weights from $1/4$–$1^1/2$oz will cover the vast majority of legering situations. These are readily available in the shops. Unfortunately, there is not a good range of shapes. The Arlesley bomb shape is readily available but I find that it rolls too easily on fine gravel. If you stick it in a vice and file or grind two sides flat then it is much better. The flatter you make it, the less it will roll and so I keep a variety. Modern non-toxic bombs are often quite horrifically shiny. This was brought home to me one sunny day when I was using one on a very shallow run. It shone out like a beacon and looked very unnatural indeed. Luckily, it is a simple matter to colour them with a permanent

A coloured, flattened and ordinary leger.

marker pen and this could mean the difference between spooking or not spooking a big fish.

Feeders are superb bait delivery systems that ensure that fish are attracted near to the hookbait. Several different types are available but the two main categories are open-ended and block-ended. Some modern forms allow the angler to vary the weights and many are also a nice dull colour. Like legers, they can be coloured with permanent markers if you find that they spook fish.

I use block-ended feeders for maggots and open-ended feeders for particles like hemp and corn. Their main disadvantages are that they can impede the strike of a light rod because of their weight and bulk, they cause a huge splosh when they enter the water and they get hung up in weed, debris and snags. I much prefer to use a straight leger if I can and feed with other methods.

FLOATS

I carry a lovely float box packed with an enormous variety of floats but in reality I only use a few of them for barbel. My favourite trotting swims are mostly 3–10ft in depth with a medium pace and clean gravel bottom.

To present a bait trundling down the run, a stable float that can carry enough shot on, or near, the bottom is required. Wire-stemmed Avons are superb for this and a range from three no. 4 to six AAA suffices.

BITE INDICATORS

You can either see, feel or hear a fish taking your bait. You can see a float going under, a rod top or quiver moving, a butt indicator rising or falling or the line moving between rod top and the water; you can feel the line tension changing when you touch leger; you can hear an electric alarm. Which of these is most suitable for barbelling?

When legering or swim feeding the main difference between bite indication on rivers and lakes is the problem introduced by the river's current and the material carried in it. The permanent and variable pull of this current in swims occupied by barbel and the variety of bites that they

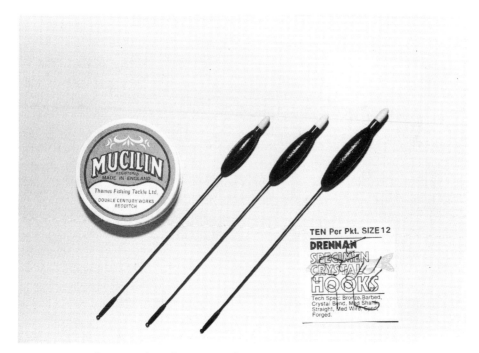

Wire-stemmed Avons, line floatant and Drennan Specimen Crystal hooks which are excellent for presenting maggots to barbel.

produce, means that a versatile system is necessary and also one which permits the angler to distinguish between the pull of a fish and the pull of a floating lump of weed.

Unless you lure barbel into calm, bank-side slacks, audible electric alarms are useless. Even if you use a line clip on the rod to stop small pulls setting them off, it is a crude and restrictive method of fishing. In fact, butt indicators of any kind do not work well for most barbel legering, unless, of course, you are using a bolt rig and so are just waiting for a fish to hook itself.

Rod-top and quiver-tip bite indication is quite good and an observant, experienced angler can usually distinguish between movement caused by biting fish and that produced by other sources. If the angler then supplements this visual information by holding the line by the reel and detecting changes in line tension, then it is even better. Touch legering is discussed more fully on page 107.

When I expect subtle barbel bites I use quivers. If the rod I have got for that particular session does not have one built-in, the Drennan screw-in type with a range of test curves from 1–2½oz is very versatile.

For night fishing, a weak isotope can be attached to the end. Strong ones can be very bright and may dazzle your vision.

WEIGHING GEAR AND RETENTION EQUIPMENT

I have a set of Avon scales, a 24 × 24in weigh bag and a sheet of thick material to lay my barbel on while I unhook them. Avons are quite accurate but must be zeroed when supporting a small weight of about 2oz. If zeroed without supporting a weight, they may be inaccurate. They also need checking regularly and so it is worth taking them to the Department of Trading Standards every close season. For a small sum, the DTS will analyse their accuracy and give you a short report.

Methods of retaining barbel are a perennial source of contention and will be discussed later in the book. For short periods, while I get my photographic gear ready, I keep them in the river in the landing net. I also have a Kevin Nash barbel tunnel available if I ever feel the need to retain one for longer but so far I have never used it. Keepnets should never be used for barbel.

BITS AND PIECES

The following list of items are essential pieces of equipment which I carry whose use is either self-explanatory or discussed elsewhere in the book.

black beads   torch
Drennan rings   bait dropper
Berkely swivels   polaroid sunglasses
link swivels   catapult
forceps   baiting needle
various boxes   PVA thread
photographic equipment
notebooks and maps
club membership books and Water Authority Licences
permanent marker pens (brown and green)
towels

*Special lights: a 6in fluorescent tube for illuminating quiver
tips and a headlamp which is useful for hands-free
operations like gathering lobworms.*

Modern SLR and compact cameras.

SPECIAL ITEMS

I regard two items of my gear as special and both are tremendously useful. The first is a small compass. This is not to help me when I get lost but to tell me exactly what direction a particular bank or fishing position faces. Once logged in my notebook I then know what swims will be most comfortable to fish during a force 8 westerly.

The second special item has probably contributed more to my own safety than any other. It is a pocket, digital, maximum and minimum thermometer with a 3m waterproof probe. Not only does this provide essential information on water temperatures but it allows me to dangle the probe in the water from a safe position instead of having to scramble down a treacherous muddy bank to perch perilously by the water's edge while I dunk a mercury thermometer in at arm's length. During a session the probe can be left in the river and you can learn whether the temperature is rising or falling and the rate at which it is doing so.

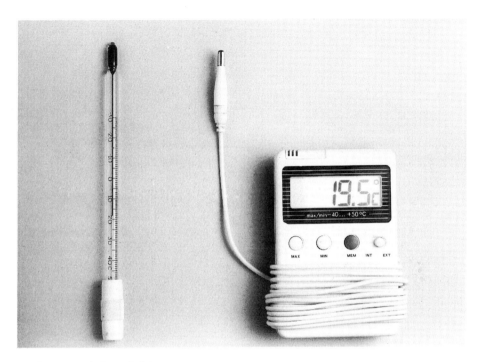

Ordinary and digital thermometers.

SEATS

Three seats are needed for all the different types of barbel fishing: a low, comfortable one for legering, a relatively high, upright one for float fishing and a light, waterproof cushion for roving. The tackle industry has produced an enormous variety of products on which to stick your rear so these days, whatever your shape, weight and requirements, you will probably find just the thing for you.

Seats with adjustable legs are useful because most river banks are sloping. It is also worth keeping as low a profile as possible in order not to scare your quarry.

In flood conditions, when your favourite spot is covered in a foot of water, long-legged seats are needed or one of those aluminium fishing stations used by the matchmen. Do not underestimate the importance of a good seat because you will not fish effectively with a numb bottom or aching back.

ROD CARRIERS AND RUCKSACKS

I never use a traditional rod holdall because my rods are always made up at home and ready to go. All I need is something to cart the brolly, rod rests and landing net and so Terry Eustace's 'Brolly Rest Sling' is perfect. It is one of the most useful pieces of equipment that I have ever bought. Wychwood tackle have recently introduced a similar product designed by John Wilson and called the 'Quiver'. This also has room for a couple of rods made up with reels on and is absolutely brilliant for roving.

Some sessions require a lot of walking and carting of quite a weight of equipment around. This can play havoc with your back and actually reduce your will to rove about. Modern back-packers' rucksacks are the answer. These are very expensive but I think they are worth their weight in gold. Features to look for are an anatomically curved suspension system, an adjustable back system so that you can set the thing up for your own back length, padded shoulder and waist straps, a detachable waterproof liner and several different zipped compartments. If you get yourself one of these you will wonder how you ever managed without one because they are so

A modern fishing station that will keep you and your equipment out of the water during floods.

comfortable. Much of the weight is supported on your hips and you can carry masses of tackle, bait and groundbait miles further than you could with a conventional single-strap fishing bag.

CLOTHES AND BROLLY

An angler who is cold, wet, uncomfortable and miserable is unlikely to fish effectively. If you are warm, dry, comfortable and happy, you will fish harder, longer and better

Despite the weight I always carry a brolly about if there is a possibility of rain. Waterproof clothes, thermal undies, Balaclavas and moon boots are all essential to defeat foul weather and keep you on the bank and fishing efficiently.

A good system is a warm and waterproof one-piece suit under which a fisherman's waistcoat is worn. This provides you with protection from the elements and also room to store all the gadgets that you need close at hand. Waders are superb for getting out to runs for trotting and legering and are also very useful for playing fish when you need to get downstream to extract them from weed. Unfortunately, they are absolutely foul things to wear if you are going to walk along several miles of bank and if that is the case, a good pair of hiking boots will keep the blisters at bay.

Baits and Bait Delivery

THE PERFECT BAIT

Traditionally, baits have been selected for barbel on their convenience. Human and animal foodstuffs have been experimented with and some have proved to be very successful. Carp anglers have changed all that, however, and now a full range of materials is available so that an angler can make his own 'customised' baits, designed for a particular species and purpose.

The perfect bait for barbel should have the following characteristics:

1. A strong water-borne scent that will stimulate barbel to search for it and then take it.
2. An appearance that will be visually recognised as potential food.
3. A taste and texture that will be recognised as food.
4. No toxic substances within it or lack of nutrients so that, if fed on exclusively by barbel, no harm will be done to them.
5. A texture to help mounting it on a hook and that will not impede hook penetration on striking.
6. A high density so that baits and feed will not be swept away by the river currents but will lie firmly on the bottom.
7. A malleability or texture to enable different sizes and shapes to be either moulded or cut. Round baits, for instance, roll out of position in a current and so flat ones are preferable.
8. It will never satiate the fish by filling their guts and so prevent them from feeding.
9. If barbel learn to avoid it the flavour or colour can be easily changed.
10. It will be very cheap and easy to obtain.

In comparison with carp fishermen, barbel anglers have been very conservative in their use of baits. There are probably several reasons for this but two may be the most relevant. Firstly, barbel seem to take a very long time to recognise new baits and pre-baiting campaigns are often unsuccessful.

Secondly, barbel either do not seem to learn to avoid standard baits as rapidly as carp, or if anglers introduce enough feed it seems their fear will be overcome. Some fish get caught season after season on the same offerings.

These factors have meant that instead of devoting time and effort to bait chemistry, it may well be best to concentrate on using common baits as efficiently as possible. Obviously, the perfect bait for barbel does not exist. Some baits are much better than others, however, and in this chapter the merits and disadvantages of each are analysed. For convenience, the classification adopted is similar to that used by the carp men.

PARTICLES (SMALL BAITS)

The five main particle baits that have been very successful for barbel are maggots, casters, hemp, sweetcorn and tares. Particles seem to be excellent baits for stimulating barbel to feed and luring them out from areas of shelter. For example, during a hot sunny day and in a low, clear river barbel may be packed under weed beds. A few dropper or swim feederfuls of maggots, for instance, may well get them out on to a gravel run. Sometimes, particles also get barbel to feed on other baits like luncheon meat if these have been ignored when fished on their own. I believe that they are a very visually stimulating bait but hemp also seems to draw fish upstream with its scent. Hemp also works very well in combination, the best known being hemp and corn as feed with corn on the hook.

Another advantage of particles is the ease with which they can be used. They are simple to mount on the hook and to feed with a dropper, feeder or loose, by hand, in shallow swims. However, droppers and feeders can be disadvantageous when barbel become scared of them and they can get caught up in weed and other snags.

A major disadvantage, particularly with maggots, is that other fish find them very attractive and so consume them and interfere with barbel fishing. Many a barbel man has travelled miles to a water, spent pounds on bait and licences only to be plagued by minnows, dace and eels. If you are lucky, though, this can bring unexpected rewards and many a 2lb roach, for instance, has been taken on corn intended for barbel.

In general, most particles have a reasonable density and once on the river bed will stay there. Maggots are probably the lightest of the group and many are wasted when they are washed away by the current. Two pints fished properly in a slackish area are better than a gallon squandered in a torrent.

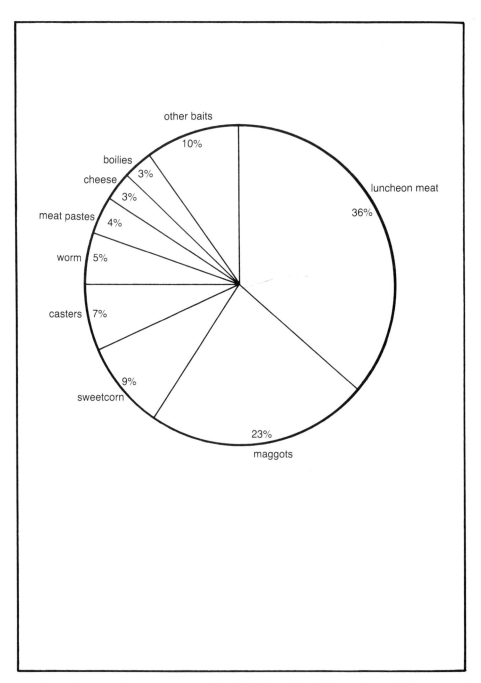

Pie chart showing the percentage of double-figure barbel caught on different baits and reported to the angling press during the 1987–8 and 1988–9 seasons.

Particles are also limiting in that it is difficult to bury a hook in many of them and so bomb a bait through dense weed. They are best fished on open areas of gravel.

All in all, particles are a convenience bait. They are easy to get, they are quite easy to use and they will lure barbel into swims that are easy to fish. They are extremely successful baits and have accounted for some huge catches and huge fish.

TRADITIONAL SPECIALS

Cheese, luncheon meat, chopped ham with pork, sausage meat and bread have all accounted for a great many barbel over the decades. They have a great many advantages. Convenience is one and each can be obtained seven days a week from grocers' shops. Years of use has meant that these baits will be recognised as food by most barbel populations but this also means that some fish will be scared of them.

Unfortunately, a great many other fish recognise them as food as well. This can sometimes be overcome by using pieces of $\frac{3}{4}$in diameter but it seems that no bait is too big for chub. Eels are also a nuisance but the smaller ones can be discouraged with a big tough bait.

The appeal of these baits is both visual and chemical. They will draw fish upstream but are not, in my experience, as effective as particles at stimulating fish to feed. These baits work best in conditions and at times when the barbel are very willing to feed. They are good night and flood baits and will also take fish if you can present them in areas of shelter where the barbel feel secure.

The texture of these baits makes them easy to cut or mould into the desired shapes and also easy to mount on the hook. Care has to be taken with some of the meats because lumps of gristle may cover the hook point and impede penetration on the strike. It is probably best to fish these baits 'hook out' with the point uncovered.

The density of this group varies enormously. Cheese and sausage pastes are fine but some brands of luncheon meat and chopped ham with pork actually float on the surface. If you find a good brand then stick to it. Never use a new type without testing it first. Bread can have the density you desire depending on the way you present it. Paste will sink quickly but flake and crust will not.

Low density in a bait can sometimes be used to your advantage. Such baits will roll along the bottom and collect in sheltered areas like slacks.

This means that if you use a light rolling leger, then the feed and hookbait should be in the same position.

To summarise, this group makes excellent baits when fished in the right locations and conditions. They are cheap and easy to buy and use. Their main disadvantages are their attraction to other fish and lack of appeal at certain times.

MODERN SPECIALS

There is some evidence to suggest that fish will learn to avoid foods that do them harm and learn to select foods that are of high nutritive value. Carp anglers have been influenced by this research and have designed baits of high protein and vitamin content. At one stage, many thought that carp could identify the protein content of a bait to within 5 per cent! Two things are certain. Firstly, more research must be done on the subject by qualified fish biologists. Secondly, high nutritive value baits (HNV) have accounted for a great many fish.

My favourite bait during high-water and night sessions.

Barbel are omnivores and so feed on a wide variety of different foods in nature. They need sources of protein and fat (largely derived from animal foods), carbohydrates (largely derived from plant foods) and vitamins. Any HNV bait should take this into account because if introduced in quantity it may be fed on exclusively by the fish.

Many excellent base mixes are available from your tackle shops or through mail order companies. You must bear in mind that you need a heavy or dense mix in rivers. A light bait will be washed away in an instant. The light ingredients to avoid are sodium caseinate, calcium caseinate, milk powders, daphnia, shrimp meal and peanut meal. The caseinates are light and the others are oily which makes them buoyant. Heavy ingredients which should be incorporated in a bait intended for barbel include ground pasta, ground rice and semolina.

The feature of these 'designer baits' that is extremely useful to the barbel fisherman is their adaptability in texture and form. You can vary the size, shape and texture of them easily. For instance, if you want a very tough bait that will deter nuisance fish and will stay on the hook as you bomb it through dense weed, then simply add eggs to the mix and boil your baits.

There are a number of base mixes that have caught barbel. One simple mix is 5oz salmon fry pellets, 4oz ground rice and 1oz wheat gluten. Proprietary baits that have also succeeded are Catchum Seafood Blend, Master Meat Mix and Fish Mix and Terry Eustace's Fish Bomb.

If you are going to use HNV baits then you should have a good reason for doing so. I would only use them in special circumstances when I could not catch on conventional baits. Most certainly, more research is needed before conclusions can be drawn about the selection of nutritious baits by barbel.

FLAVOURS AND COLOURS

Barbel have highly developed senses of taste and smell that are used to locate, identify and select food. Dozens of water-soluble flavours are now readily available to fishermen and can be added to particles, traditional specials, modern HNV baits and also groundbaits.

So far, the savoury flavours like salmon, shrimp, meat and crayfish have proved effective but so have sweet ones like honey. Believe it or not, luncheon meat and cheese flavour has also resulted in fish on the bank! The decision you must make is whether to try and use a flavour that will immediately result in food recognition or an entirely new flavour to fool a fish or shoal that has 'seen it all before'.

I always introduce free bait samples for barbel.

Bait colour will not matter at night because no fish can see in the dark. During the day the influence of bait colour will depend on the experience of the fish you are after. If they are subjected to heavy angling pressure they may associate yellow or pink baits with danger because of capture on corn or luncheon meat. Similarly, white maggots may scare them. In these circumstances, it may pay to try other colours like green. Populations and individuals that have hardly ever seen a bait are unlikely to be spooked by colours so you may as well use bright ones to aid location.

NATURALS

Lobworms, crayfish, slugs, lamprey larvae, elvers and other small live and dead fish have all caught barbel. Lobs are the best known of this group and in bygone days were used in their thousands by anglers on the Thames and Trent.

Modern barbel men neglect natural baits and this is probably because of the effort required to collect them. Why spend two hours in the middle of the night collecting worms when you can pick up a few cans of meat from the corner shop or bag of 'boilies' from the freezer? Lack of availability is, to some extent, countered by ease of use and effectiveness. Most naturals will be instantly recognised by barbel as food and they will not require much, if any, loose feeding to educate them. Unfortunately, naturals will also be well received by such nuisances as eels and jack pike. In fact, to use worms or deadbaits at night in some rivers is sheer madness.

I use naturals when I cannot catch with either particles or specials, if I am stalking a big fish and think that any other bait might spook it, or when I am using a second rod. Other situations also call for a natural bait. Lobs are extremely good flood baits and trotted minnows have caught fish in early summer.

All in all, naturals are a much neglected group of baits, particularly when you bear in mind that some evidence suggests that the older and, therefore, larger barbel, may become increasingly predatory.

LOOSE FEED AND GROUNDBAIT

Correct feeding of your swim may make all the difference between success and failure. Do it right and you will stimulate them to feed, keep them

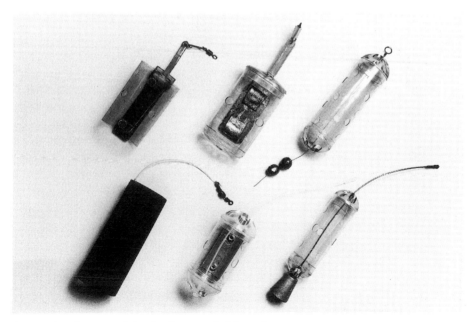

A sample of some of the feeders available today.

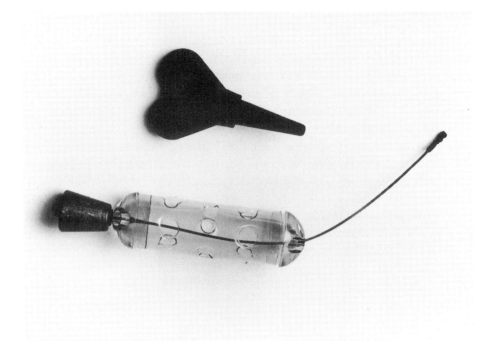

*A John Roberts' feeder hole enlarger and a small feeder with
modified release holes.*

feeding and lure them into areas of the river where it is easy to present a bait.
Do it wrong and you will scare them, fill them up or even accidentally bait
someone else's swim and so lure them away from yours.

The proper method of feeding will depend on the type of bait and swim.
Shallow swims can often be loose fed by hand if they are not too fast,
although care still needs to be taken if your bait is a light one like maggots or
bread. Bait delivery systems are necessary if there is any danger that
loose-fed bait or groundbait will be swept away from your swim by the river
current. In reality, this is in most of the situations that you are likely to
encounter.

Droppers are useful and are commonly used when trotting gravel runs.
Virtually any bait can be placed in them but they are a nuisance to use, get
caught up in weed and sometimes scare the fish. Block-end and open-ended
feeders are superb delivery mechanisms for barbel fishing. They are particularly useful for particle baits, the open-ended variety being used for the seed
baits and the block-end ones for maggots. These items double as a leger and
so anchor your bait where you want it and deliver the feed close to it. Like
bait droppers, their main disadvantages are that they may scare fish and

may get hung up in weed or snags. Another is that the holes which they are manufactured with do not allow maggots to escape fast enough in cold water. Sometimes, they become completely clogged with maggots which means that no feed is entering the swim. In such circumstances, the holes have to be enlarged. The tool to do it with is the John Roberts' 'Feeder Hole Enlarger' – a simple little device that enlarges the holes in seconds. If you find that your bait is escaping too fast, you can close some holes by wrapping waterproof insulation tape around the feeder.

Delivering special baits accurately used to be difficult, but then the 'stringer' was invented. Baits can be threaded on PVA string or thread which is attached to your leger. You then simply cast the set-up into the swim and wait for the PVA to dissolve. Unfortunately, in quite cold water of below 10°C this may take quite some time and, on occasion, I have reeled in a stringer that has not released its baits after half an hour in the river. This is unacceptable to me and so I now use what I call the 'striker'. This consists of a simple loop of 8lb line with two knots at one end. Baits are threaded up the loop with a needle, secured with bread flake pinched on the knots and the loop attached to the link swivel of the leger. The striker is cast into the swim

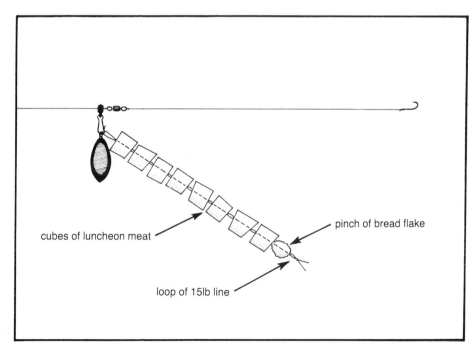

cubes of luncheon meat

pinch of bread flake

loop of 15lb line

Striker.

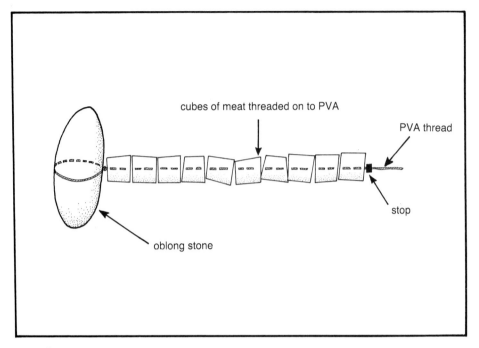

Meat baiting rig.

and after a delay of about a minute, in order to allow the flake to soften, the baits are pulled off the loop with a firm strike. The loop of line is removed for future use when you reel in. The 'striker' is very simple, cheap and effective.

PVA stringers are very useful when baiting up swims. Thread your baits on the stringer, tie it to a quite a heavy stone and throw it into the swim. When I rove the length of a fishery I sometimes bait up several swims like this at the start of the session.

Traditional groundbaits are still effective for barbel and even more so when a flavour is added to them. Good-quality breadcrumb with some added ground hemp and salmon fry crumb has helped me to catch a lot of barbel. It can be delivered in droppers or swim feeders and also by hand with a stone in the middle to make it sink quickly and hold bottom before breaking up.

DETERRING NUISANCE FISH

Other fish are attracted by the feeds introduced for barbel. If they are specimen roach or 5lb chub I can tolerate this but usually they are minnows, bleak, dace and eels. Surface feeders can be lured away from your bottom baits by loose feeding maggots, bread and small pieces of groundbait on the surface of the river. Eels are more of a problem and on some nights I just stick on a smaller hook and bait, catch them and stick them in a bag to be consumed at my convenience back home.

The alternative strategy is to use baits of at least one inch in diameter. However, I have discovered that there will always be something other than barbel around that will manage to eat them. Chub in the 2–3lb bracket are major culprits and deterring them seems impossible. The only tactic that I can suggest is to catch them and transfer them to another swim.

Barbel can also be a nuisance when they shoal because you may want to try and catch the largest in the group. Preventing the smaller individuals from taking your bait can be a problem but if you can see the shoal you can always try spreading feed over a wide area of river bed. This may have the effect of scattering the shoal, thus enabling you to cast a bait near to the big fish that you have set your sights on.

BAITS FOR BIG BARBEL

Analysis of the baits used to catch the double-figure barbel reported to the press over two years, springs no surprises. Such statistics always need very careful interpretation and although maggots and luncheon meat account for the most specimens this may simply reflect the fact that more anglers of the type who report their fish use meat and maggots. There is no doubt, however, that these two baits do take a lot of big fish.

One interesting point to note is that 'boilies' account for very few big barbel. That compares with a figure of almost 100 per cent for big carp reported to the journals.

Techniques and Tactics

One of the first decisions to be made before starting to fish is whether to sit tight in a swim where barbel are known to live or can be attracted to, or to go in search of fish with a roving approach. Whatever swim or swims are finally decided upon, the angler has then to select the method of bait presentation. Personal preference dictates what happens on a great many occasions. For example, some men will remain in a good swim and trot all day simply because that is what they like doing.

DO NOT SCARE THEM AWAY

No fish will feed if it feels in grave danger. Barbel can detect anglers by sight, sound and through vibrations transmitted from the bank and through the water. They may also be able to sense anglers if baits are tainted in some way. It has been said that the smell of nicotine may prevent fish taking.

The majority of good swims are at close range and so a very stealthy approach is needed. Keep low and use cover, do not bellow to your mates and tread lightly on the bank. Ignore cut-outs and fishing platforms if they are right next to the river and sit well back. All this advice is, of course, common sense, but common sense is not always common practice. Some people still thunder along to their swims, stand right on the skyline and drop a ton of equipment down with a bank-shuddering crash. After that, a booming voice informs anyone within a five-mile radius that a stonker of a swim has been found. The swim may have been a good one, but after all that commotion the barbel will have probably cleared off to someone else's.

Some anglers do everything right and then blow it when they hook a fish by leaping up from their swims and engaging in other manic behaviour. This not only scares away all the fish that you have been feeding but may make whatever you have hooked fight even harder.

Do not forget that at night you must be as stealthy as during the day with the added precaution of careful torch use. Once you have spooked your barbel you make it ten times harder for yourself to catch them. All it takes is a little care and thought.

THE ROVING APPROACH

Roving is my favourite tactic and it has resulted in some great catches. It is particularly suitable when you need to cover a lot of water or when you can see the barbel. When you first visit a fishery an enormous amount can be learned from dropping a bait into every likely swim – much more than just by looking at them. Ten minutes in twenty-four swims builds a better picture of a water than a quick stroll along the bank and four hours in one.

Some river stretches do not contain many barbel. In conditions when they are probably already feeding it is best to go and find them as sitting it out in one spot may be fruitless. Your bait may be 100 yards from a feeding fish. Use this strategy when the barbel are likely to be packed into specific types of swim and life will become even easier for you. For instance, a warm winter flood is just the time to rove about dropping a worm or chunk of meat into bank-side slacks and eddies.

Keeping low to avoid spooking the fish.

For roving, a rod, net and small bag of equipment are all that is required.

A minimum of clobber is essential. The more gear you cart about, the less likely you are to pick it up and move to the next swim. Leave virtually everything in the car and just take rod and reel, landing net, cushion to sit on, bait, weighing gear and bits and pieces like spare legers and hooks. What you need is just enough tackle to ensure that you can present a bait effectively in any swim you encounter. If you can stow all this stuff in a coat, leave your rucksack behind.

STALKING BARBEL

Watching a barbel creep up to a bait is one of the most exciting situations in fishing. Many is the time I have frozen, with bated breath and trembling hands, as a big fish has done this. Stalking barbel can also be an education in itself because you learn so much about their habits and feeding behaviour.

Polarising glasses are, of course, vital for seeing through the surface glare of the river. So is a period allowing your eyes to get accustomed to seeing into the water. Spend at least five minutes in every swim that you investigate analysing what you can see. Often, you will suddenly recognise a fish that was not apparent to you until you had been looking at it for some time. This is definitely a skill. Some anglers are a lot better at it than others and this is usually derived from many hours of stalking.

Several of the very best specialist anglers around at the moment spend more time wandering the banks and fish spotting than they do with a bait in the water. Reconnaissance is never wasted.

SITTING OUT A SWIM

Some fisheries get too crowded for roving and on some occasions barbel need to be coaxed with feed for a period of time before they will take a bait. In these circumstances it is probably best to settle in a swim that you know holds fish and to steadily feed it throughout the session. If, for example, you can only fish a crowded water at the weekend and it turns out too bright and sunny with the river low and clear, you will do best to get a bed of particles out.

If you cart this amount of tackle about you are less likely to move from swim to swim.

This approach is also preferable if you want a relaxing trip and can do without the strain that you get when roving from swim to swim. One fishery I know has eight extremely awkward fences to negotiate if you want to fish the entire stretch. After a week's hard work you cannot blame some people for not wanting to do this sort of thing. It can also be rather risky and I have lost count of the trousers I have ruined on barbed-wire fences, not to mention some nasty scratches to the undercarriage.

LEGERING

Barbel are mainly bottom feeders and the vast majority are caught on baits legered on the river bed. The use of a leger enables the angler to either anchor or roll a bait into a position where it is likely to be found by feeding barbel. Legers also provide casting weight and assist bite indication. If they are unsuitable they may snag up in weed or other debris, spook fish and inhibit setting the hook when you strike.

There are a number of different techniques to be mastered and problems

A fish hooked while legering in the Hampshire Avon.

94

to be overcome if a barbel man is to be able to leger a bait in any variety of swim that he might encounter.

The Stationary Leger

Sometimes, it is best to get your bait in position and leave it there for quite some time. This is particularly true where you suspect that the barbel may need to inspect it for a while before building up enough confidence to take it.

It is worth remembering that the weight of a leger mainly counteracts the pressure of the river current on the line between the rod top and the leger. Hardly any drag is caused by the bait itself once it is on the river bed. This means that the more you minimise the length of line between the leger and the river's surface, the less weight you need in your leger. Line at right angles to the current is subjected to more drag than an equivalent length of line pointing either upstream or downstream. This causes the big problem of 'line belly' when you leger straight out into the river which interferes with bite indication and hooking (*see* diagram on page 94). The greater the distance you fish at, the worse the problem becomes and linked rigs are required to enable the angler to keep better contact with the bait.

Whenever I can, I leger upstream or downstream and at as close range as possible in order to minimise 'line belly' problems. Longish rods can help when they are held high and so lift the line above the pull of the river. Upstream legering is a particular favourite of mine because the barbel can be approached from behind and baits can be dragged easily over the river bed into the exact position I want.

Legering in Weed

Barbel love weed. The angler who can efficiently leger a bait on gravel under dense weed will consistently outfish the man who sticks his bait on open gravel runs with no cover.

To get your bait under the weed you can either roll it under after casting on to a gravel run or you can bomb a bait through it with a heavy leger. Smooth heavy legers are required so that they do not get caught up in the swaying fronds of the river plants. Weights upwards of $1\frac{1}{2}$oz may even be needed if the weed is particularly dense and threatens to dislodge your bait from the river bed as it moves with the current.

What I do is to watch a weed bed for a while and try to spot any openings through it. Then I overcast upstream of the required position and quickly but gently drag the rig down and across the water's surface to the right spot. As soon as it is in position I then release line and the rig plummets to the bottom. Sometimes, it takes several attempts to get a bait on to the gravel and the way to make sure that it has is by dragging the leger a few inches with a pull from the rod top. The jagged feel of gravel is unmistakable as is the soggy pull of weed. I never leave a rig in the river if I think it is stuck in weed. If there are any doubts in my mind, I recast.

DEFEATING FLOATING WEED AND DEBRIS

One of the most maddening situations that can ruin a day's barbel fishing is when weed and other floating debris keep getting caught up with the line, constantly dragging your rig out of position. Unfortunately, such conditions often coincide with the best times for barbel to feed, such as warm

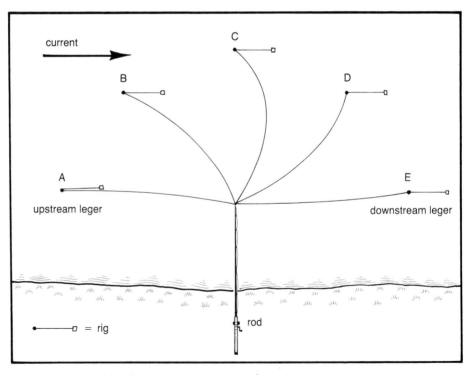

Line belly caused by the river current – it is least problematical when legering immediately upstream or downstream.

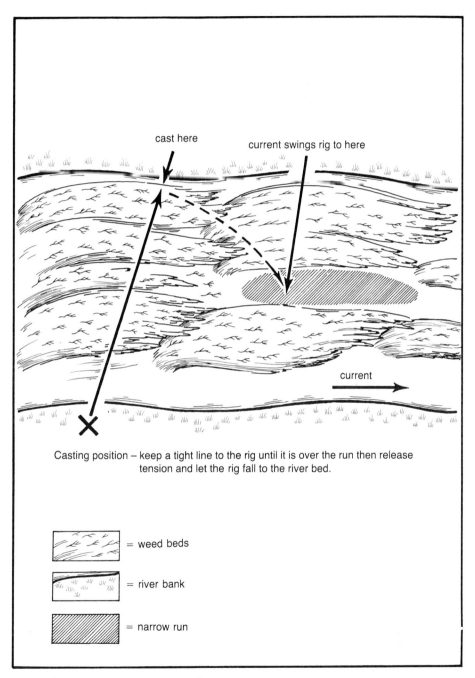

Using the river current to swing the rig over a narrow run.

floods. Weed cutting by river authorities and river keepers can also produce vast amounts of drifting muck which, when at its worst, can actually make people abandon fishing for the day!

You can either try to avoid the drifting material by fishing swims where little of it seems to collect or you can cope with it. Sheltered swims seem to be few and far between and may not be good for barbel anyway.

To cope with it, you must try to ensure that hardly any gets caught on your line in the first place. This can be achieved by minimising the length of line between rod top and leger. Fish at as close range as possible and hold your rod top underwater as far as is practicable on the day. Some debris will still get caught up in the line and so you may also have to use a heavier leger than normal. This may sound like a lot of effort but believe me it works and I have caught a lot of big fish doing exactly this.

One last point to make about this problem is to suggest that you do not

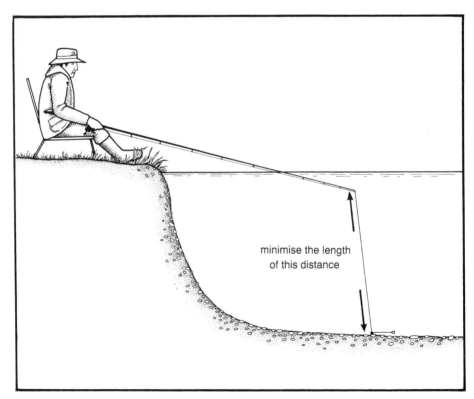

minimise the length
of this distance

Angler holding a rod under the river surface in order to avoid debris building up on the line.

Using two rods in parallel on buzzer bars.

try to use two rods. It is hard enough to fish like this with one rod; to use two would be insane.

TWO RODS IN RIVERS

When conditions are reasonable and you have a swim with a regular flow you can easily use two rods for barbel. What I do is to wrap two buzzer bars with cloth and rest my leger rods in parallel on them. The rods can be arranged so that the tips almost touch and so you will not miss any bites.

Sometimes, an extra rod is more trouble than it is worth. This is especially true when your baits are subject to the attentions of masses of nuisance fish. However, on waters where few barbel occur or where they are very difficult to catch, an extra bait in the water can be a good idea. I like to have one fishing particles and the other presenting a special of some kind.

LEGER RIGS FOR BARBEL

Different rigs are needed to fish efficiently in the many different barbel catching situations that you encounter. The main variations concern:

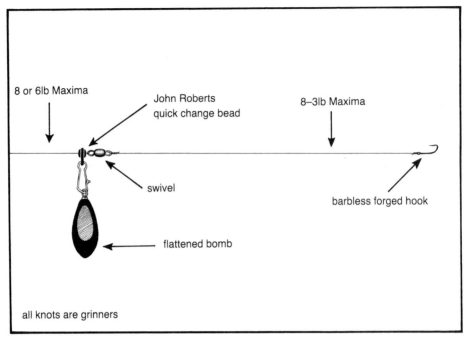

8 or 6lb Maxima

John Roberts
quick change bead

8–3lb Maxima

swivel

barbless forged hook

flattened bomb

all knots are grinners

Standard leger rig.

1. Type and weight of leger or feeder.
2. Length of trail between leger and hook.
3. Size of hook and line strength of trace.
4. Length of link to which leger is attached.

These variations are needed to prevent spooking fish, to assist the positioning of your bait in the river or to help hook the fish when you strike. The diagrams demonstrate several different rigs which have proved to be successful in specific circumstances.

Modern bolt/hair rigs are used by some anglers to catch barbel but I believe that such methods are not within the true spirit of angling. To my mind, an angler seeks to skilfully present a bait with a hook in it so that a wary, wild fish takes it. The hook is then set by striking after the bite is detected.

TROTTING

The most enjoyable method of catching barbel is to get them on the float. Trotting particles can be especially deadly but unfortunately in order to

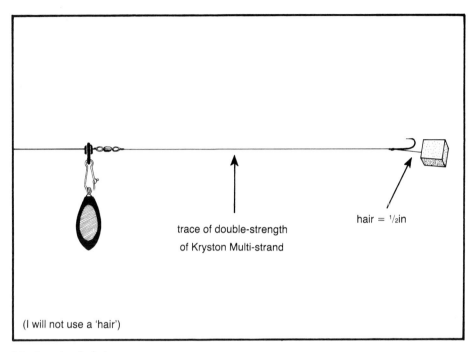

trace of double-strength
of Kryston Multi-strand

hair = ¹/₂in

(I will not use a 'hair')

Modern barbel rig.

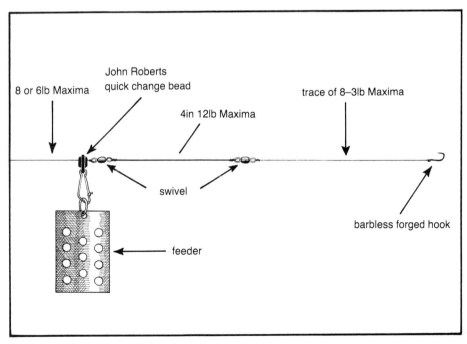

John Roberts
quick change bead

8 or 6lb Maxima

trace of 8–3lb Maxima

4in 12lb Maxima

swivel

barbless forged hook

feeder

Standard feeder rig.

present a small bait well, light tackle has to be used and so some fish may be lost. I hate losing barbel so I do not trot as often as I would like to.

Maggots are the most popular trotting baits but casters, hemp, corn, flake and tiny pieces of luncheon meat all catch a lot of fish. Classically, a clean gravel run is fed with a dropper and a bait is trundled over the river bed with a float fished double rubber, overdepth and held back. With a good rod and decent centrepin this type of fishing is sheer delight. Bites are usually dramatic; the float disappears and stays under.

I have had most success trotting in the warmer months of the year and I suspect that this is due to the barbel themselves being more willing to move to food quickly when their bodies are warm. The key to success seems to be in the feeding of the swim. A dropper or half dropper full of hookbait before every single trot down should get them feeding. Try and watch someone trotting and feeding a shallow swim and observe the barbel. You may be amazed at how they tear about chasing the feed. No feed and they just lie doggo watching the hookbait waft past.

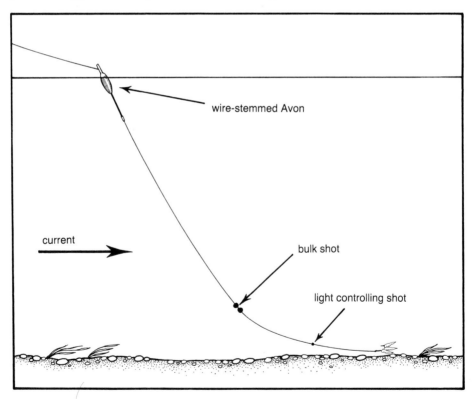

Trotting rig.

Trotting with a big centrepin is my favourite way of catching barbel.

OPPORTUNISM

Successful barbel fishing is all about being in the right place at the right time. Although this sounds very obvious it is easy to ignore. What I rarely do is say, 'this coming weekend I'm going barbel fishing'. What I normally say is, 'this coming weekend I'll go barbel fishing if the weather is right and the river looks good'.

Planning and organisation are vital but restrictive long-term planning that ties you to one type of fishing is not. What you need is to have tackle, bait and transport ready so that as soon as conditions are perfect you can get on the bank and have a bait in the water. This will depend on work and family commitments but do not fall into the trap of thinking that every fishing session has to be four or five hours long. One hour in the right conditions is worth twenty-four in the wrong ones. These 'grab sessions' can be fitted in before work in the morning, on the way home from work in the evening or first thing on a Saturday before you dive off to help with the shopping.

My gear and bait is constantly ready and every day I monitor tempera-ture, rainfall and wind direction. As soon as I like what I see, I get down to

103

the river. It helps to have the rod set up with reel on, line threaded and rig attached so that when you arrive at the river you just bait the swim, put the landing net up and cast in.

One last word about swim selection. Every session, if only for ten minutes, stick a bait in a swim that you have never tried before even if it looks grotty. You may be surprised. I always try to remember to do this and although I often draw a blank I sometimes hit the jackpot. The best example I can give of this is one particular session at the Middle Avon. One shallow swim that I had totally ignored for two years produced five barbel in consecutive casts!

Getting Them on
the Bank

BITE DETECTION

When a barbel takes a legered bait it will approach it, perhaps test it with its barbules and lips, test it again by taking it into its lips and then take it further into its mouth before swallowing it. All this can take place rapidly, in a second or so, or can extend over quite a period of time.

The angler may detect all of these things, firstly with a 'line bite' as the fish hits the line, then vibrations as the barbel tests the bait and finally, a firm pull as the confident fish takes the bait in. The procedure is more complicated if the leger moves over the river bed because this will cause additional

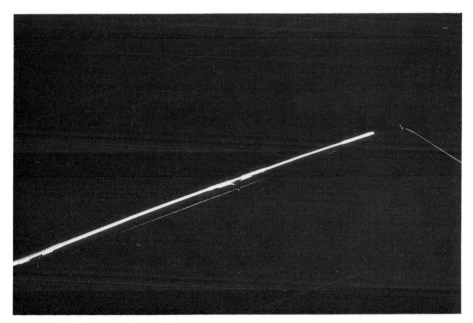

A quiver illuminated with a lamp.

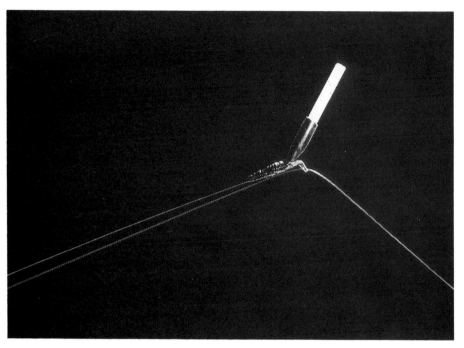

An isotope on a quiver.

vibrations. False bites may also be recorded from variations in river current, swaying weed and drifting muck.

All this information is transmitted to the fisherman along the line and will register either as an increase in tension or a decrease in tension. If you are upstream legering or legering straight out from the bank you may get slack line bites or a series of vibrations as your leger or feeder moves over the river bed. Any bite indication system should allow the identification of the various components. Those available include the visual signals of rod top, quiver tip, butt indicators and monkey climbers. There are also audible electric alarms and the sense of touch when holding the rod and line.

At night, watching a rod top or quiver can be done by using an isotope, a torch or some source of light in the background like street lights or a bright moon. If you choose to try a torch, use one of the short fluorescent tubes. They emit a glow in which it is easy to position your rod top or quiver. This restricts you to fishing with your rod top low down and a couple of feet from the bank but it is the best artificial source of light I have yet discovered for this purpose. Most of these torches take four AA size batteries which last for hours.

In my experience, to rely purely on visual signals does not help to identify, for example, the pull from a fish or the pull from a drifting leaf. A quiver may pull round an inch, a monkey climber may rise or fall an inch but what exactly does that mean?

I combine the senses of sight and touch and rely on rod top or quiver plus the tension of the line on my fingers. This combination is deadly but to describe the difference in feel between the pull of a fish and the pull of weed, for example, is difficult. A real bite feels 'alive' or 'electric'.

This method is also versatile and will work in any swim. You try setting up an Optonic and monkey climb system in a fast weedy stretch of the Hampshire Avon. It may work in circumstances where the problems of current and muck are absent but you will be restricted to these swims. Despite saying all this, on stretches where bites are very few and far between, there is a lot to be said for feeding an easily fished swim, setting up a pair of rods and waiting for the alarm to go off.

Another advantage of the sight and touch combination is that you will detect some subtle bites from wary barbel that would not show up on other systems. This method requires a lot of concentration but when mastered it will bring rewards. I read recently that one author would never touch leger because it results in premature striking and foul hooking! This is nonsense.

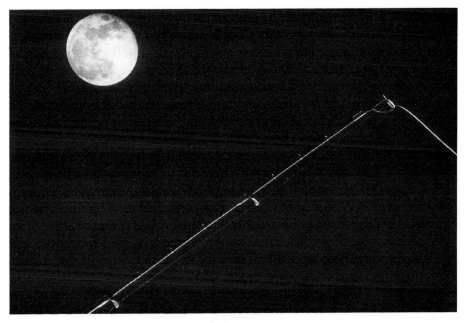

A rod top held up against the moonlight.

Concentrating on a quiver.

Cold winter weather can cause the problem of numb and insensitive hands. You really must try to keep your hands as warm as possible and now, after many seasons of touch legering, I have found that wrapping a large clean towel around my hand and reel beats any pair of gloves. It looks a bit peculiar but it works a treat because you can still strike easily. The towel just falls off when you start playing the fish.

STRIKING AND HOOKING

I only strike when I think that the barbel has finished testing the bait and has it inside its mouth. This is usually signalled by a prolonged increase in line tension. I think that the duration of the pull is more important than the extent and I strike if the rod top has been pulled round half an inch for two or three seconds. Slack line bites are more difficult to interpret and I hit those as soon as I feel the leger move. Too light a leger will move too early and so it is important to use enough weight to resist small plucks, but not too much to either spook the barbel or prevent me from controlling the bait.

The word strike might not be appropriate because what really occurs is a fast, firm pulling of the hook into the fish. If the strike is snatched you run the risk of snapping the line.

PLAYING AND LANDING

How you play a barbel will depend on the tackle you are using. If you have 8lb Maxima direct to a big forged hook you can take more liberties than with 3lb line to a size 14.

Playing a fish starts before you hook it. Analyse each swim for potential problems and gear up accordingly. There is absolutely no point, for instance, in hooking a barbel at 40 yards downstream on fine line and then expecting to haul it up river through dense weed. If you have a snaggy swim, use heavy gear and always make sure your landing net is within reach of the spot you choose to land the barbel.

Make full use of the curve of the rod to protect the line and hook-hold and do not get 'pointed' through loss of concentration. 'Pointing' is when you let the rod point towards the fish so that a sudden lunge is taken directly by the line and hook, increasing the risk of breakage or pull out. The most critical time is when the barbel is just in front of you and you reach for the net. A great many good fish are lost within inches of being landed. I imagine that this is when a fish sees you for the first time and you may be applying

A well-positioned landing net is near at hand.

just that little bit of extra pressure to get it in. You then glance down at the net, reach for it and drop the rod slightly, the barbel makes a lunge for the safety of the river bed and 'snap' it is gone. To eliminate this sort of disaster, it helps to make absolutely sure that the landing net handle is just by your foot. The slightest loss of concentration may lose you your barbel.

Never use less than 5lb line if the swim contains weed and you cannot walk below the fish after hooking it. If you can get below it, do so because you must pull downstream to get barbel out of weed. If a barbel gets stuck in weed, do not panic, just wait. What I do is get below the fish and maintain light pressure of about a pound on the line. Sooner or later the fish begins to kick and then I increase my pull. In the end, the fish itself seems to clear a path out. Never be tempted to go in for a fish if the river current is powerful and you are unsure of the depth. Sometimes, you have to strip off and go out to release a barbel that is stuck fast. One school of thought maintains that if that is the case then the fish has won the battle. Although this is a very valid point of view, I would rather not leave a fish with a hook in it and trailing a length of line.

Sometimes, barbel are hooked near snags and have to be held out as soon as they are hooked. Soft rods may bend enough to allow them to get into

110

their refuge but you can reduce the 'give' by holding the rod in the middle with a hand and walking backwards to pull them away from the danger. You had better make sure that you know what is behind. I will never forget one of my mates doing this and stepping straight back into a very deep and muddy ditch. You also need to be pretty confident in your rod because they are not built for this treatment and may snap.

Barbel fights vary. The biggest fish usually fight quite slowly and powerfully and hug the river bed. Smaller barbel, of about five or six pounds, fight like tigers and rush all over the place. Whatever size you have hooked, try to land your fish quickly because if it becomes exhausted it will take a long time to recover. Try fooling it with light pressure and you may be able to lead it to the net. One thing is certain and that is, if you start giving it stick, it will pull back even harder.

CARING FOR AND RETURNING BARBEL

I would never fish if I thought that I could not return what I caught, unharmed, to the river. Barbel are particularly prone to damage by anglers

A badly positioned net may cause a loss of concentration.

Applying side strain to keep a barbel out of weed.

for two reasons: one of the horny dorsal fin rays is serrated and gets caught up in coarse-meshed nets, and they become exhausted easily.

Soft-meshed landing nets are needed and keepnets should not be used on these fish. If you must retain one, use a barbel tunnel made out of material and when you lay it down on the river bank put it on a piece of thick material or polythene to protect it from abrasion on stones or gravel.

It seems to be a barbel's nature to fight hard. If you allow barbel to, they will fight themselves to exhaustion and so strong tackle and proper fighting technique will get them in quickly. They become exhausted because they have relatively little 'steady swimming' muscle and a lot of 'sprinting' muscle. The essential difference between these two muscle types is that sprinting muscle uses up its energy reserves quickly and takes a long time to recover. An exhausted barbel will, therefore, take a while to build up its strength in order to maintain itself in the river current without getting washed away. If you return a very tired one to a fast stretch of water, it may be doomed to drift off downstream.

Unhooking, weighing, photography and general admiration should be accomplished as quickly as possible. I can remove a barbless hook and get a fish weighed very quickly. If I am going to take a photograph I then put the barbel back in the landing net and immerse it in the river (head pointing

Increasing the pressure on a fish by pulling from well above the handle.

upstream, of course), while I get the camera equipment ready. When all is arranged, out comes the fish, off goes the camera and I am ready to release it.

When letting your catch go, hold the barbel in shallow medium-paced water until it starts to breathe steadily and begins swimming motions with its body. Only when you think it has recovered its strength should you let it go. If you see it float, belly up, and start to drift downstream make every effort to net it and start helping its recovery all over again.

Barbel are magnificent creatures that provide many people with great pleasure. I regard it as an absolute duty to do all I can to look after them.

The Barbel Season

For me, the barbel fishing season is divided into summer, autumn and winter because during these three periods river conditions and, therefore, barbel behaviour gradually change. This necessitates a corresponding change in fishing tactics to ensure that fish are still caught and fruitless sessions are avoided.

Summer, consisting of the months June, July and August, is characterised by low clear rivers, abundant weed and warm temperatures. Rain storms occasionally raise and colour the river waters but the extent of this varies from year to year.

Autumn conditions prevail during September, October and November. During these months, water temperatures gradually fall, the weed slowly dies off and increased rainfall elevates the flow and clouds the water with suspended sediment.

In winter, barbel fishing is dramatically influenced by the weather because during December, January, February and March temperatures are at their lowest and river conditions fluctuate from one extreme to the other. One week the banks can be covered in snow, the waters will be low, gin clear and freezing cold; then, following warm westerly winds and torrential rain, the rivers will be muddy, belting down, over their banks and warm.

During this chapter the best strategies and tactics for each part of the year are discussed and examples given of how they have been successfully applied in various sessions. If you think that my memory for detail seems remarkable, do not be fooled – I keep very comprehensive fishing diaries which extend back twenty-three years! The examples are taken from a variety of seasons. There were many other very successful sessions in between and also my fair share of blanks.

SUMMER

Hot sunny weather in June, July and August and low clear rivers favour particle baits, stalking fish and trotting through clear gravel runs. At night, and after rain, meat and natural baits are also deadly and so summer, for

me, is characterised by hemp, sweetcorn, maggot and caster sessions inter-
spersed with opportunist outings after rain with the other baits.

Fast weedy stretches often contain the largest shoals of fish and it is
during this period that time spent fish watching to locate the biggest barbel
can bring rewards.

Throop Fishery – July

During one of my summer holidays at Throop, I spotted a shoal of very big
barbel above the New Weir. Secrecy was vital on these vacation trips
because Rosalie Guest House, where I stayed, was always full of mad keen
and very competitive young anglers. One careless sentence would mean that
the spot would always be occupied by a rival.

The swim in question was a fast and deep run on the outside of quite an
acute bend. About ten feet of tanking Stour belted over clean gravel
bordered by dense streamer weed. Three big fish could occasionally be seen
on this run but they were very wary. If I stuck my head too far over the bank
in order to get a better view, they melted into the weed immediately.

Watching a barbel swim up to a bait is incredibly exciting.

I estimated the size of the trio at 6lb, 9lb and 10lb. My biggest barbel at the time was about seven pounds so I am sure you can imagine the way my heart pounded and fingers trembled whenever one of the big ones inspected my bait. Inspect was all they did do, at first, when I started with meat and cheese but then they became very spooked at the mere sight of these baits so I had to rethink my tactics.

A feeder packed with maggots got them interested again and a bait dropper also helped introduce quantities of feed, however I still had to suffer the frustration of watching them mop up all of the loose maggots and totally ignore the hookbait. I also noticed that they did not like getting too near to the feeder and would hang back at least a yard, waiting for maggots to trundle down to them. Again, tactics had to be rethought and so the trail was increased to six feet, the trace line was brought down from 6–4lb breaking strain and a 12 hook replaced the size 10.

Holding my breath I lowered the new rig on to the run and can vividly remember seeing the smallest fish start to mop up maggots and then suck in my bait. Without waiting for a pull, I struck and the fish shot upstream, burying itself in the dense weed. Ten minutes later the Avons pulled round to 8lb 14oz, a personal best at the time and cause for due celebration at one of Bournemouth's many night-clubs – not that we really needed an excuse to go to one.

That near-nine-pound fish I had estimated to weigh 6lb, so my mind boggled at the possible size of the others which dwarfed it. Twelve-pounders-plus they must have been but despite trying on several occasions I never got them to accept a bait.

The next year, the swim was destroyed when Wessex Water started its imaginative dredging of the lovely Stour. Where those big barbel went, I will never know.

Middle Hampshire Avon – July

On one hot sunny day I was having a great time trotting maggots on the River Nadder near Salisbury when suddenly it clouded over and the heavens opened. A summer storm started to lash the Wiltshire countryside and after a while I noticed that the river was on the rise and was starting to colour.

Without more ado, the trotting gear was chucked into the van and I sped off southwards towards an Avon fishery near Fordingbridge. The stretch was a very hard one and you could fish it for a week without seeing a barbel.

Waiting for the pull of a big barbel.

However, despite this 'degree of difficulty', the weather and river conditions had me brimming with confidence.

The swim I chose was pretty fast, about five feet deep and about as weedy as they come without being totally unfishable. It was just about possible to swing a rig round in the current and then bomb a heavy lead through the swaying fronds on to the gravel.

Before tackling up, I catapulted about thirty chunks of meat well upstream of the run so that they would sink and trundle down with the current. The gear was my favourite 10ft Avon, Mitchell Match, 8lb Maxima, size 4 Au Lion d'Or 1534 and flattened Arlesley bomb. One ounce of leger weight was needed to drag the bait down through the weed and keep it anchored on the run. Bite detection was nigh on impossible because the dense weed constantly pulled on the line. Holding the rod and feeling the line was vital as was total concentration.

My diary says I managed about six casts before reluctantly complying with the 'no night fishing' rule of the club who rented the fishery. I landed barbel of 9lb 8oz, 9lb 7oz and 8lb 15oz on three of them and lost a good fish on another. At the end of the session I was soaked to the skin but very happy. Such a catch was unheard of on this particular water and I was also delighted that my tactics had been proved correct.

Middle Avon – July

One season I was working so hard that I had not managed a single barbel trip until mid-July. Then it poured with rain one day and so I leapt into the car knowing that a lump of meat legered in one of my favourite swims was likely to produce the goods.

Opportunism is a very efficient way of catching fish if you know your waters like the back of your hand and have supreme confidence in your methods and tackle. It certainly paid off on this occasion because the two-hour round trip and two hours on the bank produced a beautiful fish of 11lb which is a lovely way to open your account for a season.

Middle Avon – August

A period of blazing summer weather had lowered the Avon and made it as clear as gin. A particles session was called for and so I boiled up a load of hemp, emptied umpteen corn cans into a bucket and set off on the hour-long journey to the lovely Avon valley.

A nice double from the Middle Avon.

The river was warm – 20°C – so I chose a shallow run between dense weed and below gravel shallows where the water became well oxygenated as it tumbled over and over.

Several 'pult loads of hemp and corn were shot into the swim and an open-ended feeder also delivered additional feed. Almost immediately, I caught a small fish of about three pounds which is just the sort of boost you need to your confidence to start a session. Four hours later, six more barbel had hit the bank with the best going a shade over the 10lb point on the scales. It was typical particle bashing – regular feed from the 'pult and feeder kept the shoal interested and bites were positive and unmissable.

Two lost fish marred the session slightly. One good barbel had snapped the hook-link after the feeder had become entangled in weed and I had lost a lovely roach when the hook pulled out at the net. A two-pounder, possibly, which meant that I missed the chance to fulfil the ambition of a double-figure barbel and a 2lb roach on the same session.

Dorset Stour – August

To my embarrassment my diary starts the record of this trip with 'another day with a hangover'. I was working down in Dorset but had packed my gear into the car in readiness for a short evening session. The weather was foul for the tourists but great for the barbel fishermen – lots of lovely rain.

I had had a quick look at the Avon during the day but had seen the great rafts of weed caused by the weed cutting and so had chosen to fish the Stour. There was only time for about an hour's fishing so I made great haste to the swim and set the gear up in record time. Despite this it was beginning to get dark when I made my first cast with a lump of meat legered upstream almost under a bridge.

It was paradise. The lovely bridge pool was overhung by willows and surrounded by lush reeds. The rain had stopped and the evening was 'as still as death' according to my diary. Mist rose from the river and the only movement was the sway of the weed and sinuous mercurial flow of the river's surface.

Within seconds, I had a marvellous drop-back bite and a strike connected with a big fish that bore deeply into the pool – 9lb 4oz that one, which was quickly followed by one of exactly 9lb. With time left for one more cast, I heard a fish sucking at weeds at my feet. I dropped the rig on to the run next to the weed bed and seconds later was playing a fish of 7lb 8oz. On some trips everything goes right. Three casts and three lovely barbel!

Over the years I have travelled many miles for situations like this.

AUTUMN

Barbel tend to move gradually into slower stretches and swims as the temperatures fall during September, October and November. In addition, the weed starts to die back and, denied their beloved shelter, the fish often seek sanctuary in the depths and other sources of refuge. During these months my techniques are often similar to those of summer but my choice of swim changes and I am more inclined to fish two rods in a deep hole.

Middle Avon – September

This was a sociable session with Simon Lush, his mate, Stewart, and Rob Wilson, a buddy of mine from the early years at Throop. A good start was made with Simon getting lost on the way down and then being accidentally backed into a muddy ditch by a rather embarrassed me. The weather was absolutely ferocious with storm-force winds from the west and pile-driving rain. There cannot have been many people out fishing that night.

I was the only one who knew this particular fishery so I guided the others into good swims on the Avon's west bank. With our backs to the storm the fishing was not too unpleasant but I must admit to being surprised when the others called it a day after only a couple of hours' fishing. There was no way I was packing it in with a warm, coloured river on the rise so I moved into Simon's vacated swim and soon had a lump of meat legered out on the run.

Without any warning there was a sudden crack, a great whooshing noise and then a thunderous crash as a tree fell to the ground. It missed me by about ten feet and I reckon to this day that if I had been holding my rod out to my side the tip would have been broken off. You will not be surprised to learn that I had the shakes for about half an hour after that.

The extra flow had shifted a lot of rubbish in the river and it was constantly building up on the line, giving false bites and shifting my rig. To combat this, I decided to fish nearer to my bank, to cast upstream and to hold the rod tip underwater and feel the line for bites. On one cast I felt a quick pluck followed by slack line as the rig shifted downstream. I pulled into the fish and the light rod assumed a lovely battle curve as the fish hugged the bottom and set off downstream. I knew that I was attached to what might have been my first double.

It was, and at 10lb 6oz, tears of joy mixed with the rain on my face. I wanted a good photograph of this personal best so I supported the lovely barbel in my large, soft landing net in flowing shallow water and set off to rouse one of my buddies who were three-quarters of a mile away, snoozing in comfort in their cars. To my amazement, none of the swines would leave the sanctuary of their cars and I had to trudge back and photograph the fish myself.

Why did I catch that fish and not the others? My answer is simple – it was me who had the self-motivation to stay and brave the elements. Had Simon remained in the swim, it would have been him that struck gold, not that I complained at the time, however.

River Kennet – November

The most enjoyable way to get barbel is definitely on the float. To guide a float skilfully down a run, trundle a bait towards the fish and have the delight of seeing the float dive under and a strike meet with the solid pull of a big fish is pure ecstasy.

This particular stretch of Kennet was very weedy in the summer and it held a good head of medium-sized whiskers up to about nine pounds. On this trip in November, I found that much of the weed had gone and the fish could not be seen on the shallows so I opted for a deep bank-side glide bordered by weeds. The flow was purposeful rather than fast and I had a very strong hunch that the run was full of fish.

A depth of 6ft and an absence of too many nuisance dace and bleak meant that the run could be loose fed and I put in a couple of big handfuls of maggots as I tackled up. First trot, with the float almost scraping the reeds, I latched into a four-pounder and my heart leapt with the anticipation of a fantastic bag. It was probably one of my best ever, but exactly how good I will never know because I lost count of the fish and did not bother to weigh any except two that went over 7lb. I reckoned on about twenty fish and well over eighty pounds in total. A truly fantastic day and one I remember most of without having to resort to the diary.

Middle Avon – October

This trip turned out to be a bit of a 'fishathon' and is testament to the hungry nature of my need to catch fish. It was probably caused by a lack of fishing because my diary reads: 'Disaster! No fishing for ten days, van broken down', just prior to this trip.

On arrival at the Avon, at 6 p.m., the usual roving gear with plenty of meat baits was grabbed and I set off towards a lovely coloured river. After fishing my heart out until dawn I had eight barbel, including a double, under my belt and was 'well pleased', as they say. Five were taken on consecutive casts but the shine on that feat was dulled by the loss of a very big fish on the sixth.

Not wanting to stop for a minute, I quickly grabbed a few coffees from the Primus in the car and returned to the river armed with the trotting gear. Eight chub to over four pounds and twenty odd chunky Avon dace later I realised that I had been trotting for hours and so returned to the car for a few more cups of sustenance. Despite having had no sleep for over a day I was still raring to go and was on a fishing 'high'. Back I went with the leger tackle and managed two more barbel to 9lb 10oz before calling it a day at midnight due to fatigue.

I had fished hard – touch legering and trotting – for thirty hours without any sleep and with only a few cups of coffee to keep me going. My reward had been about a hundredweight of fish including ten lovely Avon barbel and the bonus of a double-figure fish. Needless to say, I slept pretty soundly that night but probably made reeling in and striking motions in my sleep.

Middle Avon – October

I made a mistake on this trip but was very lucky to get away with it. A big barbel was spotted in a swim that I called Clive's Dip because a friend

One of my early winter Kennet barbel.

On many of these sessions I have ended up soaked to the skin, my chair sunk in the mud and my bait boxes floating in flood water.

of mind had fallen into it one day, much, I have to confess, to my amusement.

This particular fish could be seen on a run and it was taking loose-fed maggots with gusto. I trotted several baits down without a bite and then tried lighter gear, resorting to 3lb line and a forged 16 hook presenting a couple of maggots. The fish still would not take so I went lighter still to 2lb line. That did the trick and I latched into what looked like a nine- or ten-pounder.

Then my troubles began. Although the weed had died back it was still dense and tough enough to cause extreme problems on the flimsy gear. The fish took full advantage of my lack of control and cover and so it was a full half an hour before I slipped a landing net under it. I had to nurse nine pounds of exhausted barbel for a very long time before it regained enough strength to swim off back into the river current. Since then, I have never gone below 3lb line because it just is not fair on the barbel.

WINTER

My thermometer is indispensable during the months of December, January, February and March. I constantly monitor air and water temperatures and wind direction. Any relatively mild spell with lovely warm rain blown in from the west gets me reaching for the barbel gear and rushing down to the river. Warm floods really get me enthusiastic and many a time I have waded across swamped fields towards a river whose banks have disappeared.

Maggots, meat, worms and bread are my favourite baits for this period of the year and they are always presented on the bottom with leger or feeder because I have never caught many barbel trotting in winter.

River Kennet – January

This session occurred about twenty years ago and was the first on which I caught a winter barbel. It was a fluke because I was really after chub but that little fish of about two pounds really opened my eyes because up until then I thought that they could not be caught after November.

I have no idea why I fished this particular stretch in Reading because the far bank was packed with a row of terraced houses and while I fished I had to listen to people shouting and screaming at one another. I am glad that I did persevere, though, because I ended up catching quite a few barbel from the water that winter and so was firmly launched as a winter barbel man.

Middle Avon – January

The country had been in the icy grip of a big freeze with temperatures down to a miserable −11°C. The *Angling Times* and *Angler's Mail* were absolutely devoid of any fish reports and so it seemed that nothing was being landed throughout Britain. Then the weather broke with westerly winds bringing rain and air temperatures of 12°C. The Avon rose from 4°C to 8°C and I had an eight-hour session in a favourite slack by a bridge. Six barbel took my legered chopped ham with pork with the best going 9lb 15oz. I actually won a carbon rod from the *Angler's Mail* for that fish which just goes to show that not much else was being caught. Normally, I would not have got a look-in with a fish of that size. I did not complain.

Middle Avon – March

The Bat and Ball at Breamore was my home for a week as I holidayed in Hampshire for the last week of the season. The weather was very kind and the river was in magical form being high, warm and coloured. Over the first few days I had had several lovely barbel from a deep bank-side slack but had not latched into anything big. Lobworms had been the killing bait and I spent an hour or so every night gathering them from the pub lawn together with my friend, Dave Howe. Dave and I would fish hard all day and then rush back to the pub in the evening for a fabulous hot meal washed down with several pints of ale.

On the fourth day of the week, Dave decided to drive down to Christchurch to investigate the potential at the Royalty. I decided to persevere on the Middle Avon Fishery because I knew that it contained very big fish. At about lunch-time I was fishless but still full of optimism. To my surprise, Dave suddenly appeared and it transpired that the Avon was so flooded that it was totally unfishable lower down. I was just about to reply, 'nothing', in answer to Dave's, 'Have you had anything?' when the rod dipped as my lob was taken. A strike latched into something that felt quite horribly immovable.

After ten minutes I hadn't even got it off the bottom let alone seen it and that was on quite a powerful outfit with 6lb line. Dave was looking worried. At one stage I got the fish virtually under the rod top in about five feet of water and, despite bending the rod double and getting the line to sing in the wind, I couldn't shift the fish an inch. It felt huge.

I then suffered probably one of the most sickening things that can happen to any fisherman – the hook pulled out. Only people who have experienced this sort of thing can appreciate the mind-numbing agony that accompanies the loss of such a fish. I definitely lost something very special that day.

Middle Avon – February

This was another opportunist trip in response to warm weather but after three hours' fishing a 'cert' swim I had not caught. This was very frustrating because I knew that the fish would be there and taking the bait if it was put in front of them.

My tactics were upstream legering into a deep hole below some quite fast shallows. Because of my failure I shifted my position to 10 yards above the hole and rolled a bait down the gravel shallows and into the hole. Almost immediately I had a take and landed a fish of 10lb 7oz. It had been there all along but it took a precisely positioned bait to get it.

A shot which captures the atmosphere and concentration of my barbel sessions.

SUMMARY

Over the very many years that I have fished for barbel I have landed quite a few decent fish. If there is one personal attribute which has contributed to this more than any other it is determination. I have fished hard, very hard, in fact, and have persevered in spite of cold, hunger, failure and antagonism from others. A good biological education has helped enormously but it is time on the bank with a bait in the water that counts. Woody Allen once said '80 per cent of success is showing up'. This is very true of fishing.

Other Species

Although barbel are my first love, other fish also figure heavily in my season and chub, mullet, pike and roach all get me reaching for the tackle. This chapter certainly is not meant to be an extensive treatise on how to catch these fish but is meant to describe how they can be fitted into a campaign that concentrates on barbel.

In certain weather conditions when barbel are difficult, if not impossible, to catch it is more sensible to go after fish that are more willing to feed. Even when barbel are feeding, it is often worth giving a swim a rest for an hour or two and wandering down the bank to look for other quarry.

*A surprise carp from a barbel swim on the
Avon.*

A big river chub.

CHUB

In general, I start to think about chub fishing in two situations when I think that it may be hard to get a few whiskers on the bank. Firstly, in blazing hot summer conditions and, secondly, in freezing cold winter weather. Big chub generally occupy swims of slower current speed than barbel and also require more delicate tackle to fool them – 3lb and 4lb lines, smaller hooks and compulsory quiver tips to detect chub bites which can be so tiny that they can easily be missed. My two biggest fish hardly moved the tip at all. It is often necessary to ignore the tip altogether and just watch the bow in the line from river surface to tip.

In the summer, stalking chub is a great way to spend the afternoon when the barbel are not interested in feeding. If ever you need a stealthy approach it is when stalking a big chub. These fish seem to be able to detect the tiniest movement on the bank and they can just melt away into the weed never to be seen again on that session. Particles are brilliant stalking baits as are natural baits. On the majority of waters I have found that common baits like meat, cheese and bread are totally blown out for big chub and if you get one of these baits anywhere near a fish it bolts in terror. Cold winter conditions are great for chub and terrible for barbel. Trotting and quiver tipping with bread will get you plenty of fish and the important thing to remember is to stick plenty of mashed bread and free pinches of flake into the river.

MULLET

My mullet fishing started, by accident, when I spotted some huge fish in Christchurch Harbour where the Hampshire Avon meets the Dorset Stour. They were massive, with the biggest looking like it wasn't too far short of double figures.

These fish feed in shoals which line up, side by side, and, like grazing cattle, move slowly over the bottom mopping up algae and other food items. Hot summer weather is good for mullet and they feed well in the evening when a 'stepped-up roach fishing' approach works well. I caught a lot by spreading out a carpet of mashed bread and corn and fishing with two quiver rods. Mullet bites are infuriating. Most are short plucks and pulls and you may well only hit one in ten. If you are after big fish do not fish too light because they fight harder than barbel. I would never go below 4lb line and a size 12 hook. You had better have plenty of line on the reel as well

Playing a river pike.

because they make very powerful runs. Trotting bread is another good method for getting mullet and you do not miss so many bites.

If I lived nearer the sea I would definitely give up some barbel fishing time to go after these fish – they are brilliant.

PIKE

I will go after river pike if I spot a good one in the summer or in winter when the rivers are low, cold and clear. Deep, slow or still bank-side slacks are great river pike swims.

A great method to get them is to rove along a stretch of river at dawn or dusk with a minimum of tackle and to put a bait into every likely hole for five or ten minutes. I like sardines because they are soft, very smelly and can be easily obtained in decent sizes. They are too soft to cast easily to the far bank of many rivers but if you are fishing under your own bank they are great.

Fishing a pike slack in winter.

Legering for barbel in the same swim at dusk.

Powerful equipment is vital for these fish because river pike fight like tigers. Many swims produce more than one fish so if you get one do not move on straight away.

Good river pike swims have sometimes proved to be good winter barbel swims as well and I have taken both on the same day by deadbaiting during daylight and then legering meat after dusk.

ROACH

Many a specimen roach has been taken by a barbel man when using particles and many a barbel has been hooked on flimsy roach tackle. They seem to occupy very similar swims during summer, autumn and winter.

I think that big roach are fantastic fish and I often sacrifice barbel fishing time in order to get them. An excellent combination is to trot for roach during the day and then leger for barbel during the night.

In winter floods, the timing of roach and barbel fishing can vary. I have found that barbel will feed avidly when the river is on the rise and at the

A good river pike.

A beautiful big roach.

Another fantastic big roach – one of the few fish that I will sacrifice barbel fishing time for.

height of a flood when it is chocolate coloured and carrying loads of muck. Roach do not feed nearly as well during these conditions but really come on when the river is fining down and clearing. By this time the barbel may have gorged themselves and so it is a good idea to get out the light roach tackle.

On the Hampshire Avon, where masses of bread is piled into the river by roach fishermen, this bait catches barbel. What seems to happen is that bread wafts downstream and collects in slacks where barbel mop it up. I have caught quite a few on big chunks of flake legered on a size 6.

Index

Other fishing books published by The Crowood Press

Match Fishing – The Winner's Peg *Paul Dennis*
An instructional, anecdotal journey through a match fishing season with some of Britain's leading match fishermen.

Angling Afloat – A Complete Guide for Coarse Fishermen *Stephen Harper*
The first book devoted exclusively to freshwater boat fishing which will appeal to newcomers as well as experienced boat anglers.

Grayling – The Fourth Game Fish *Ronald Broughton*
Grayling experts give details on methods, tactics, tackle, locations and recount personal anecdotes.

Perch – Contemporary Days and Ways *John Bailey and Roger Miller*
Suggests alternatives to standard methods of fishing for perch, describing more exciting and successful innovative tactics.

In Wild Waters *John Bailey*
A book which inspires enthusiasm for wild water fishing in every angler, expert or novice by one of Britain's best-known fishermen.

Reeling In *Arthur Oglesby*
Offers a unique insight into the angling career of one of the sport's giants, Arthur Oglesby.

To Rise a Trout *John Roberts*
A unique guide to the techniques and tactics of dry fly fishing for trout on rivers and streams.

Barbel *Barbel Catchers and Friends*
Every river, every method and every bait is covered with each chapter written by a man who is an expert on his water.

The Handbook of Fly Tying *Peter Gathercole*
Provides a thorough grounding in the basics of fly tying, and takes the novice to a point where he or she is able to tackle even the most tricky methods.

Travels with a Two Piece *John Bailey*
A collection of writing inspired by the author's journey along the rivers of England with an ancient two piece fly fishing rod.

River Fishing *Len Head*
How to read waters and set about catching the major coarse fishing species.

Boat Fishing *Mike Millman, Richard Stapley and John Holden*
A concise but detailed guide to modern boat fishing.

Stillwater Coarse Fishing *Melvyn Russ*
A guide to the maze of tackle, baits, tactics and techniques that surround the cream of coarse fishing in Britain.

Beach Fishing *John Holden*
A comprehensive insight into the fish, their habitat, long distance casting, tackle, bait and tactics.

My Way with Trout *Arthur Cove*
Outlines the techniques and tactics employed by the master of nymph fishing on stillwaters.

In Visible Waters *John Bailey*
John Bailey reveals the deep insight that he has gained over nearly thirty years closely observing the lives of coarse fishing species.

Imitations of the Trout's World *Bob Church and Peter Gathercole*
Describes advanced fly tying techniques and explores the link between the natural and the artificial.

Bob Church's Guide to Trout Flies
Covers some 400 flies, with advice on how to select the right one and how to fish it.

Fly Fishing for Salmon and Sea Trout *Arthur Oglesby*
The first recent really comprehensive work to deal almost exclusively with fly fishing techniques.

Tench *Len Head*
Natural history, physiology, distribution, tackle, tactics and techniques are discussed in this most comprehensive study of the species.

Pike – The Predator becomes the Prey *John Bailey and Martyn Page*
Twenty top pike angler's experience of all types of waters.

Carp – The Quest for the Queen   *John Bailey and Martyn Page*
Combined specialist knowledge from twenty-six big fish men.

Long Distance Casting   *John Holden*
A guide to tackle and techniques of long-range casting in saltwater.

The Beach Fisherman's Tackle Guide   *John Holden*
Covers rods, reels, accessories, rigs and maintenance.

An Introduction to Reservoir Trout Fishing   *Alan Pearson*
Covers tackle, casting, flies, bank and boat fishing, and location.

Rods and Rod Building   *Len Head*
A manual of rod building, giving guidance on design and the selection of rods.

Further information from **The Crowood Press (0793) 496493.**